Transforming Novices into Professionals

Transforming Novices into Professionals

A Comprehensive and Systematic Guide to Teacher Induction

Matthew J. Jennings

ROWMAN & LITTLEFIELD
Lanham • Boulder • New York • London

Published by Rowman & Littlefield
An imprint of The Rowman & Littlefield Publishing Group, Inc.
4501 Forbes Boulevard, Suite 200, Lanham, Maryland 20706
www.rowman.com

86-90 Paul Street, London EC2A 4NE, United Kingdom

Copyright © 2022 by Matthew J. Jennings

All rights reserved. No part of this book may be reproduced in any form or by any electronic or mechanical means, including information storage and retrieval systems, without written permission from the publisher, except by a reviewer who may quote passages in a review.

British Library Cataloguing in Publication Information Available

Library of Congress Cataloging-in-Publication Data

Names: Jennings, Matthew, author.
Title: Transforming novices into professionals : a comprehensive and systematic guide to teacher induction / Matthew J. Jennings.
Description: Lanham, Maryland : Rowman & Littlefield, 2022. | Includes bibliographical references. | Summary: "Transforming Novices into Professionals is the ultimate resource for conducting a systematic and comprehensive multi-year teacher induction program"—Provided by publisher.
Identifiers: LCCN 2021023118 (print) | LCCN 2021023119 (ebook) | ISBN 9781475861921 (cloth) | ISBN 9781475861938 (paperback) | ISBN 9781475861945 (epub)
Subjects: LCSH: Teachers—In-service training—United States. | Teachers—Professional relationships—United States. | Mentoring in Education—United States.
Classification: LCC LB1731 .J397 2022 (print) | LCC LB1731 (ebook) | DDC 370.71/1—dc23
LC record available at https://lccn.loc.gov/2021023118
LC ebook record available at https://lccn.loc.gov/2021023119

Contents

Acknowledgments		vii
Preface		ix
1	Introduction	1
2	Year One: Classroom Management and Professionalism	11
3	Year Two: Direct Instruction and Professionalism	35
4	Year Three: Classroom Assessment and Professionalism	59
5	Year Four: Teacher Action Research	73
6	The Role of Mentoring in the Induction Program	87
Appendix		97
References		105
About the Author		107

Acknowledgments

I want to thank my wife, MaryAnn Jennings, for her help with the formatting of this text. I would also like to thank my daughter, Tara Jennings, for her proofreading and revision suggestions. Lastly, I would like to thank Anthony Ruela for his content suggestions. Without the help from each of you, this book would not have reached the level of quality desired.

Preface

Millions of new teachers are projected to enter US schools in the next decade. Are schools prepared for them? Considering the positive causal relationship between the quality of teaching and student achievement, answering this question must be of critical importance to educational leaders. If our students are to reach high levels of academic achievement, we need to hire, develop, and retain highly effective teachers.

All teachers begin as novices. Novice teachers are those that have demonstrated the basic level of readiness to independently serve as the teacher of record in a classroom. However, due to their lack of experience, novice teachers do not have the knowledge of teaching and learning possessed by their more seasoned peers. Furthermore, while novice teachers may demonstrate high levels of enthusiasm, they simply cannot be expected to have the same skill set as more experienced teachers. Expert performance is acquired slowly over a very long period of time. In fact, the highest levels of performance and achievement appear to require at least ten years of intense preparation (Ericsson, 1996).

Unfortunately, many novice teachers will not stay in the classroom long enough to acquire this level of skill. According to Smith and Ingersoll (2004), as a result of feeling overwhelmed, ineffective, and unsupported, 15 percent of teachers leave the profession after their first year and 14 percent change schools. Estimates for the exodus of teachers within the first five years are approximately 30 percent. Even more troublesome is the fact that the most talented new educators are often the most likely to leave (Gonzales & Sosa, 1993).

For those who choose to stay, high rates of teacher turnover may have significant negative effects. A chronic and large influx of new teachers is likely to have a negative impact on school health and climate (Guin, 2004). High staff turnover disrupts program planning and implementation processes and requires repetition of professional development opportunities. In short, chronically high teacher turnover adds a significant degree of chaos and complexity to schoolwide operations, potentially harming student learning across classrooms and teachers (Laitsch, 2004).

The combined exodus of new teachers and the negative impact on the teachers who choose to stay leads to the conclusion that we are not ready for the millions of new teachers expected to join the profession. We must make a choice; we can train and support new teachers so that they stay and thrive, or we can let them fend for themselves so that they leave or struggle to survive.

Teachers who feel supported and have some initial success are much more likely to remain in teaching. In addition, how well a new teacher is trained during the first few years of teaching influences how effective they will become (Breaux, 2016). Schools and districts require comprehensive, systematic induction programs that facilitate teachers' transition from novices to professionals. The content of this book, combined with the content found in *From First Year to First Rate: Thriving during the Initial Years of Your Teaching Career* (Jennings, 2021), provides the structure and materials needed for this type of program.

Whereas *From First Year to First Rate* focuses on building the domain-specific knowledge required for effective teaching, this book focuses on practices that reflect on that content. Regular, structured teacher reflection improves pedagogical skills (Marzano et al., 2012). Teaching is a skill and, like any skill, it can be improved through focused practice and quality feedback.

The goal for this book is to combine this value of reflection on performance with the introduction of content essential to effective teaching. Through the use of the activities in this book, the growth of a novice teacher's knowledge and skills will be accelerated. In addition, the mindset of reflection as a deliberate effort to improve performance will be established.

This book is intended for all personnel who administer staff induction programs. In small districts that may be the building principal and in larger districts that role may be assigned to the central office. Regardless of setting, this induction program can be implemented. It does not require substantial funding or extensive resources. However, it does require administrative commitment and time for reflection and collaboration. Through the implementation of this induction program, educators will be prepared to successfully transition novice teachers to the professional stage of their careers. For those teachers who come to a district with significant teaching experience in another district, the hiring administrator will need to decide if all or some parts of this program are appropriate.

While not intended to be a guide on mentoring, this book will conclude with a section on the role of mentor teachers in this induction program. Mentors cannot serve as a substitute for a comprehensive, systematic induction program. However, when selected carefully, trained appropriately, and given clear roles, mentors can greatly enhance the experiences of novice teachers.

1
Introduction

Imagine a school in which every classroom is staffed by a teacher who creates an environment conducive to learning, provides high-quality direct instruction, uses valid and reliable classroom assessments, and acts in a highly professional manner. Is it highly likely that a school composed of this type of staff would achieve significant results for students? Most, if not all, educators would agree that even a school challenged by significant external barriers would achieve significant student growth if it was composed of a staff with this type of knowledge, skill, and disposition.

Now ask yourself, can I realistically say that the school or district I work in meets this characterization? If you are like most, the answer to this question is no. Considering that these basics of professional teaching are not extremely costly or impossibly complex to master, why is this the case? At least one major reason for this situation is a lack of systematic focus on teacher growth and development. In particular, we often do a poor job of transitioning novice teachers to the professional level of teaching.

New teachers may have orientation, mentoring, and induction focused primarily on procedures. All of these supports are necessary, but insufficient. Novice teachers also require a sustained, focused, systematic program that moves them from pre-service to professional teaching. This requires time, commitment, and clarity of expectations. We must begin to think of novice teacher development as a multiyear, phased program of learning, application, and demonstration of mastery.

The foundation of effective teaching is classroom management. If a teacher cannot create an orderly, safe, positive learning environment, they will not be able to provide effective instruction. Yet, a 2004 Public Agenda survey found that 85 percent of teachers believed that new teachers are particularly unprepared for dealing with behavior problems in their classrooms. A separate survey of five hundred teachers found that teachers with three or fewer years on the job were more than twice as likely as teachers with more experience to say that student behavior was a problem in their classrooms (Melnick & Meister, 2008). Classroom management is a skill set that can and must be learned. This should be the primary professional development goal for the first year of every novice teacher.

With a solid foundation of effective classroom management established, teachers can effectively provide instruction. Obviously not all types of instruction are equally effective. Furthermore, some types of instruction are more complex than others to learn and implement. High-quality, direct instruction is a research-based and effective framework for teaching a vast array of content material. With the right assistance, teachers can learn to effectively implement this model of instruction. Learning to provide quality direct instruction should be the primary professional development goal for the second year of every novice teacher.

Instruction is only effective when it produces student learning. A professional teacher must be able to make informed decisions based on demonstrated student performance. In classrooms, these informed decisions result from classroom assessments. Importantly, the quality of these decisions can only be as good as the quality of evidence gathered. A low-quality assessment tool cannot yield a high-quality decision regarding student levels of knowledge and skills. Learning to create and use the data from valid, reliable classroom assessments should be the primary professional development goal for the third year of every novice teacher.

We often think of teachers as professionals who work in their own classrooms. While it is true that most of their work is performed while isolated from other adults, the fact remains that they are a part of a system. Teaching requires regular interactions with colleagues, administrators, parents, community members, and a variety of other adults. The dynamics of these interactions can either strengthen or weaken the system.

Someone skilled at classroom management, direct instruction, and classroom assessment can still demonstrate professional behaviors that weaken the overall quality of a school. Unprofessional behavior can contribute to faculty mistrust, cynicism, low morale, and a "silo" mentality. In this type of environment, student and faculty performance both suffer. For this reason, understanding and applying professional norms of behavior must be the focus of every novice teacher from their first day of employment.

Thus, a comprehensive and systematic induction program that moves teachers from the novice to professional stage will have the following goals:

- **YEAR ONE**—First-year teachers will demonstrate proficiency in classroom management and professional behavior.
- **YEAR TWO**—Second-year teachers will demonstrate proficiency in classroom management, professional behavior, and instruction.
- **YEAR THREE**—Third-year teachers will demonstrate proficiency in classroom management, professional behavior, instruction, and assessment.
- **YEAR FOUR**—Fourth-year teachers will demonstrate proficiency in classroom management, professional behavior, instruction, assessment, and the ability to complete a teacher action research project.

To achieve these goals will require provision of professional development, opportunities for application, reflection, accountability, and constructive, meaningful feedback. This book, in combination with the text *From First Year to First Rate: Thriving during the Initial Years of Your Teaching Career* (Jennings, 2021), forms the basis for both providing professional growth opportunities and documenting the performance of novice teachers.

HOW TO USE THIS BOOK

What follows is one proven protocol for organizing and implementing a school or system-wide approach. It is by no means the only approach, and must be modified to meet local needs and resources. Next, each component of the protocol is explained and a sample timeline for implementation is provided.

PROFESSIONAL DEVELOPMENT OPPORTUNITIES

The book *From First Year to First Rate: Thriving during the Initial Years of Your Teaching Career* (Jennings, 2021) provides the content and process for conducting a series of study sessions. In the timeline provided, the sessions are spread out over the course of three years. The focus of these sessions corresponds with the goals established for each year of the novice induction program.

The content of this book, including the application activities and discussion opportunities, provides the content required for obtaining the necessary knowledge and skills for each goal. All of the guidelines for forming these groups and the specific questions for discussion can be found in the final section of that book.

APPLICATION AND REFLECTION OPPORTUNITIES

When teachers appropriately reflect upon and use the feedback they receive from student surveys, it leads to improvement in teaching and in the educational environment for the students (Aleamoni, 1999). Thus, this book includes multiple protocols for teacher reflection including student surveys.

Student surveys focus on the means rather than the ends. As a result, they give teachers tangible ideas about what they can fix immediately, straight from the students who sit in their classrooms every day. The student survey questions used in this program accurately reflect the teaching expectations of the overall induction program. Therefore, they can and should be used to improve teaching quality. They are not intended to serve as a formal evaluation component.

Student Voice—Survey Administration

1. The teacher shall administer the appropriate student survey. There are different student surveys, each with a focus on the goal for that year. In addition, there are two versions of each survey. The content of both versions for each year are the same, but the wording is different depending upon if the students are elementary or secondary level. If the students are not able to read the survey in-

dependently, the teacher may read the statements aloud, allowing students to respond to each in turn.
2. Administration of surveys shall occur once in December and once in February. The teacher shall compile the survey results and complete the required self-reflection form. The surveys themselves remain the property of the teacher.
3. If multiple classes composed of different students are taught, the teacher shall choose one class to survey. This shall be the same class for both survey administrations.
4. The required self-reflection forms shall become a part of the teacher's portfolio.

Video of One's Own Teaching

Another powerful tool for teachers to obtain focused feedback about their performance is to watch video of themselves teaching. A number of research studies indicate that viewing such video augments teachers' reflection and performance (Armstrong & Curran, 2006; Cunningham & Bendetto, 2002; Sorenson, Newton, & Harrison, 2006). Viewing video teaching helps teachers evaluate how much their performance differed from self-expectations.

Watching video of one's own teaching is more effective when careful analysis of the video is required (Hennessy & Deaney, 2009). Thus, teachers in this induction program are required to have a specific focus for viewing and to reflect upon what they observed.

USE OF VIDEO CAPTURE FOR REFLECTIVE PRACTICE

1. Using a personal or district-owned recording device, the teacher shall record and reflect upon two lessons throughout the course of the school year. One shall be recorded in November and the other shall be recorded in January.
2. The length of the video recorded shall be a minimum of twenty minutes. The focus of the video shall be on the implementation of the strategies corresponding to the goals for that year.
3. The teacher shall watch the video and complete the required self-reflection form. The teacher is not required to show the video to

anyone, but may choose to share it with his or her direct supervisor or a peer group.
4. The required self-reflection form is another of the required elements in the teacher portfolio. There is no required video analysis for year three.

Teacher Portfolio

Teacher portfolios provide teachers with opportunities for self-reflection. In addition, they can be helpful tools for assessing teaching quality. However, to achieve these aims they must be more than a miscellaneous collection of artifacts or an extended list of professional activities. Teaching portfolios must carefully and thoughtfully document a set of accomplishments attained over an extended period of time.

In addition, it is important to carefully select the contents of the finished portfolio so that it is manageable for both the person who constructs it and the person who reviews it. The requirements of the portfolio for each year of this induction program are designed to encourage reflection while minimizing the quantity of material included.

Creating the Teaching Portfolio

1. Each teacher shall submit a portfolio that contains the following elements:
   a. Reflective writing focused on the corresponding goals of the year.
   b. Required elements:
      i. Student Survey Summary Forms 1 & 2
      ii. Teacher Video Reflection Forms 1 & 2
   c. Three choice items selected by the teacher. Different choices are required for each year.
2. The portfolio must be submitted to the teacher's evaluator in March.

Accountability and Constructive Feedback

Instructional coaching has a dramatic impact on teachers' skills. When comparing teachers who receive coaching to uncoached teachers with the same initial training, those who received coaching practiced new strategies more frequently, developed greater skills with strategies, used strategies more appropriately, exhibited greater long-term retention of strategies, and were more likely and better able to explain new strategies to their students (Joyce & Showers, 2002).

Of course, teacher observation and coaching are not always synonymous. Because teacher observation is often used for accountability, it can be perceived as threatening. Yet, effective communication can only take place in a nonthreatening environment. Administrators who coach teachers whom they also evaluate must emphasize learning and growth. The road to expertise starts and ends with small incremental steps forward. When observation is connected to teacher learning and growth, anxiety regarding accountability is greatly reduced. Unrealistic expectations are also a source of anxiety for novice teachers.

It is nonsensical to use the same observation instruments with novice teachers that we use with experienced teachers. The expectations for classroom performance should not be the same for these two groups. Attempting to evaluate the instruction of a typical novice teacher with the same instrument used with a veteran teacher will either result in an unfair poor performance rating or an inflated rating that is based on adjusted expectations. Neither of these two outcomes is valuable for providing high-quality performance feedback.

The quality of the feedback the coach provides is critical. The feedback provided should be specific and honest. In addition, it should be focused on behavior that can be changed, not the person. Specifying which strategies a teacher is using correctly and effectively, which strategies a teacher is using with errors or omissions, and which strategies a teacher should use but currently isn't will likely improve the teacher's knowledge and skill. This induction model attempts to focus on providing formative feedback prior to making a summative judgment of teacher performance.

Teacher Observation

1. Using the appropriate form, the observer will document and provide feedback to the teacher on the specified focus area.
2. Each observation form contains the subdomains and observable teacher and student behaviors that might be expected if implementation was being performed effectively. It is important to note that not every behavior will be demonstrated in every observation.

In addition, behaviors not listed may also show effective application of the teaching skill. This requires understanding of the teaching context and appropriate, informed judgment by the observer. Due to the fact that evaluation of assessment skills is primarily based on products, there is no specific observation form for year three. If observations are required for that year, one of the forms for management or instruction could be substituted.
3. Each form contains space for constructive feedback. In addition, appropriate supervisory skills should be exercised to provide additional feedback during post-observation conferences.
4. Because these observations are meant to be formative, they do not contain a performance rating.

Summative Rating Forms

1. Each domain contains a rubric-based rating scale that is to be used to evaluate teacher performance over time.
2. Observational data and teacher reflection products are combined to make a summative judgment of the teacher's performance. This summative judgment can lead to additional professional development opportunities and/or decisions regarding renewal of employment.
3. As the summative evaluation forms contain the previous year's rubrics, they are cumulative. It is expected that teachers will continue to demonstrate proficiency with previously learned skills from one year to the next.

Table 1.1 shows a possible calendar for implementing this induction program.

SUGGESTED IMPLEMENTATION TIMELINE

The next four sections provide the materials required for each specific year of the induction program. Thus, these sections are written to directly address the teacher participants. Each section begins with an explanation of the goals and activities of that year for participating teachers. The first year also includes explanations for completing each

Table 1.1. Comprehensive Induction Program Calendar

MONTH	YEAR ONE	YEAR TWO	YEAR THREE
		ACTIVITY	
SEPTEMBER	• Book Study #1—Classroom Management	• Book Study #3—Direct Instruction	• Book Study #6—Assessment
OCTOBER	• Book Study #2—Classroom Management	• Book Study #4—Direct Instruction	• Book Study #7—Assessment
NOVEMBER	• Book Study #9—Professionalism • Video Analysis #1 and Reflection Form Completed	• Book Study #5—Direct Instruction	• Book Study #8—Assessment
DECEMBER	• Student Survey Administered and Reflection Form Completed • Classroom Observation #2		
JANUARY	• Video Analysis #2 and Reflection Form Completed		
FEBRUARY	• Student Survey Administered and Reflection Form Completed • Classroom Observation #3		
MARCH	• Portfolios Due		
APRIL	• Summative Evaluation Conferences		

task and a blank set of deadlines. After the first year, it should not be necessary to provide teachers with explanations for task completion. The set of deadlines varies based on school calendars. Thus, the program administrator must decide upon the due dates and insert them in the appropriate spaces.

Next, each section proceeds to provide the teacher with the forms required to complete the activities. All of these materials can also be reproduced and made into a packet that is provided to the teachers in that cohort at the beginning of the year. It is important to review these materials with the teachers as close to the start of the school year as possible.

Each section concludes with the tools that will be used to document teacher performance. More specifically, an observation form and a summative evaluation form are provided. While it is not necessary to share the observation form in advance, it is appropriate to provide teachers with the summative evaluation form at the beginning of the school year. This further promotes clarity of teacher performance expectations.

2

Year One: Classroom Management and Professionalism

OVERVIEW OF YEAR ONE

Welcome to year one of our district's teacher induction program. The goal for this year will be for you to demonstrate proficiency in the area of classroom management and professionalism. More specifically, it is expected that you will demonstrate proficient implementation of the following district teaching standards. The teacher:

- effectively organizes the physical space in the classroom.
- effectively develops classroom rules and procedures.
- effectively and consistently reinforces classroom expectations and procedures.
- effectively and consistently uses verbal and nonverbal behaviors to develop and maintain positive, appropriate relationships with students.
- consistently demonstrates awareness of the actions of all of the students in the classroom and consistently behaves in a manner that is objective and controlled.
- effectively and consistently uses strategies to foster the understanding between effort and achievement.
- consistently demonstrates principles of professional behavior.

Of course, other aspects such as instruction and assessment remain important. However, these will not serve as the focus for professional growth and evaluation in your first year.

In order to assist you in meeting these goals, you will participate in a collegial study of the first and last section of the book *From First Year to First Rate: Thriving during the Initial Years of Your Teaching Career* (Jennings, 2021). While reading the assigned section of the text you will be expected to make annotations. This will help you prepare for each study session. In these sessions, you will participate with colleagues in the discussion of questions designed to build understanding of the content.

Additionally, you will have opportunities to obtain student perception of your work through collection and reflection on student surveys. Another opportunity for reflection will be through self-analysis of videotaped segments of your classroom performance. The student surveys, reflections of video, and other required items will be assembled into a teacher portfolio that will be provided to your lead observer.

You will have multiple classroom observations throughout the course of the school year. These observations will focus on your implementation of the previously listed standards. As these observations are intended to be formative, they will not provide you with performance ratings. Instead, you will receive constructive feedback on your implementation of the standards.

The content of your portfolio and formal and informal observations by your supervisor(s) will be combined with other relevant data to draw conclusions related to your progress. At a summative conference you will receive final ratings of your performance toward these standards. These ratings will be used to make decisions regarding additional professional development opportunities as well as continued employment in the school district.

The goal of the school district is to see you succeed. It will require effort on your part, but you will receive abundant support throughout the process. At the conclusion of this year, it is our sincere desire to see that you have established proficiency with these standards so that you are prepared to progress to the next phase of our induction program.

TASK-SPECIFIC DIRECTIONS AND TIMELINES

Student Survey Administration

1. You shall administer the appropriate student survey. Grades K–5 will use the elementary version and grades 6–12 will complete the

secondary version. If the students are not able to read the survey independently, you may read the statements aloud, allowing students to respond to each in turn.
2. If multiple classes composed of different students are taught, choose one class to survey. This shall be the same class for both survey administrations.
3. Administration of surveys shall occur twice, according to the deadlines provided. After the survey has been completed, you are to compile the results and complete the required self-reflection form. The surveys themselves remain the property of the teacher.
4. The required self-reflection forms shall be included in your portfolio.

Video Self-Analysis

1. Using a personal or district-owned recording device, you are required to record and reflect upon two lessons throughout the course of the school year. Deadlines for completing this task are provided.
2. The length of the recorded video shall be a minimum of twenty minutes. During year one, the focus of your analysis shall be on the implementation of classroom management strategies.
3. You are to watch the video and complete the required self-reflection form.
4. The self-reflection forms are required elements of the teacher portfolio.

Teacher Portfolio

1. You are required to submit a portfolio that contains the following elements:
   a. Reflective writing focused on the corresponding goals of the year.
   b. Required elements:
      i. Student Survey Summary Forms 1 and 2
      ii. Teacher Video Reflection Forms 1 and 2
   c. Three choice items selected by the teacher. Different choices are required for each year.

2. This portfolio must be submitted to the teacher's evaluator by the date specified on the list of deadlines below.
3. The goal of this portfolio is to be concise and reflective. You may not add additional elements, nor is there any value in going beyond the requirements listed.
4. You will receive feedback on the quality of this portfolio during your summative evaluation conference.

Summative Ratings

1. Your final evaluation will be based upon scores for rubrics aligned to each standard that serves as the focus for the year. The rubrics are included for your review.
2. Your evaluator will use observational data and the contents of your portfolio to make a summative judgment of your performance. This summative judgment will be used to make decisions regarding renewal of employment and may lead to additional professional development opportunities.

DEADLINES FOR TASK COMPLETION

Book Study Group Meeting #1: Date: _____ Time: _____
Location: _____
Book Study Group Meeting #2: Date: _____ Time: _____
Location: _____
Book Study Group Meeting #3: Date: _____ Time: _____
Location: _____
Video Analysis #1: Date: _____ Video Analysis #2: Date: _____
Student Survey #1: Date: _____ Student Survey #2: Date: _____
Portfolio Due Date: _____

Table 2.1. Summative Rating Rubrics for Classroom Management and Professionalism

DOMAIN 1—CLASSROOM MANAGEMENT			
SUBDOMAIN	PROFICIENT	DEVELOPING	BEGINNING
Physical Organization of Classroom	**Effectively** organizes the classroom to facilitate movement and promote a focus on learning.	Some of the aspects of the physical organization of the classroom facilitate movement and promote a focus on learning.	The organization of the classroom does not facilitate movement, nor does it promote a focus on learning.
Establishment of Classroom Expectations and Procedures	**Effectively** develops expectations and procedures to encourage positive student behavior.	Aspects of the expectations and procedures are effective, but other aspects are missing or ineffective.	The expectations and procedures for encouraging positive student behavior are neither comprehensive nor effective.
Reinforcement of Expectations	**Consistently** and **effectively** both acknowledges and reinforces positive student behavior while providing appropriate consequences for undesirable student behavior.	**Occasionally** acknowledges and reinforces positive student behavior and provides appropriate consequences for undesirable student behavior.	Neither acknowledges and reinforces positive student behavior nor provides appropriate consequences for undesirable student behavior.
Teacher-Student Relationships	**Consistently** and **effectively** uses verbal and nonverbal behaviors to develop and maintain positive relationships with students.	**Occasionally** uses verbal and nonverbal behaviors that develop and maintain positive relationships with students.	**Does not** consistently use verbal and nonverbal behaviors that develop and maintain positive relationships with students.

(continued)

Table 2.1. (continued)

SUBDOMAIN	PROFICIENT	DEVELOPING	BEGINNING
Mental Set	**Consistently** and **effectively** both demonstrates awareness of the actions of all of the students in the classroom and behaves in a manner that is objective and controlled.	**Occasionally** demonstrates awareness of the actions of all of the students in the classroom. Usually behaves in a manner that is objective and controlled.	Neither demonstrates awareness of the actions of all of the students in the classroom nor behaves in a manner that is objective and controlled.
Reinforcement of Effort	**Consistently** and **effectively** both uses explicit strategies to foster the understanding of the relationship between effort and achievement, and acknowledges students' efforts when they work hard to achieve.	**Occasionally** uses explicit strategies to foster student understanding of the relationship between effort and achievement and acknowledges students' efforts when they work hard to achieve.	Neither uses explicit strategies to foster student understanding of the relationship between effort and achievement, nor acknowledges students' efforts when they work hard to achieve.
DOMAIN 4—PROFESSIONALISM			
Respect for Others	**Consistently** demonstrates respect for every member of the organization.	There have been **isolated incidents** of not demonstrating respect for others.	**Frequently does not** demonstrate respect for every member of the organization.
Dependability	**Consistently** follows through on assigned tasks and completes promised actions in a timely manner.	There have been **isolated incidents** of not demonstrating dependability.	**Frequently does not** follow through on assigned tasks and complete promised actions in a timely manner.
Honesty	**Consistently** tells the truth with the appropriate degree of tact.	There have been **isolated incidents** of not demonstrating honesty.	**Frequently does not** tell the truth with the appropriate degree of tact.

SUBDOMAIN	PROFICIENT	DEVELOPING	BEGINNING
Accountability	**Consistently** accepts responsibility for achieving meaningful student growth over time.	There have been **isolated incidents** of not demonstrating accountability.	**Frequently does not** accept responsibility for achieving meaningful student growth over time.
Integrity	**Consistently** expresses beliefs appropriately, and models the ability to do what they believe is right in the face of challenging circumstances.	There have been **isolated incidents** of not demonstrating integrity.	Neither expresses their beliefs appropriately, nor models the ability to do what they believe is right in the face of challenging circumstances.
Risk-Taking	**Consistently** demonstrates willingness to try new strategies, and takes the initiative to learn from attempts that did not achieve desired results.	There have been **isolated incidents** of not demonstrating risk-taking.	Neither demonstrates willingness to try new strategies nor takes the initiative to learn from attempts that did not achieve desired results.
Humility	**Consistently** considers the needs and feelings of others, accepts constructive criticism, and asks for necessary assistance.	There have been **isolated incidents** of not demonstrating humility.	Neither considers the needs and feelings of others nor accepts constructive criticism. Does not ask for necessary assistance.
Collaboration	**Consistently** collaborates with colleagues in a genuine manner.	There have been **isolated incidents** of not demonstrating collaboration.	**Frequently does not** collaborate with colleagues in a genuine manner.

STUDENT SURVEY—ELEMENTARY VERSION
CLASSROOM MANAGEMENT

Date: _____ Class Period: _____

Directions: Please read the statements below. For each statement place an X in the box that identifies how much you agree with that statement. **Do not write your name on this survey.** When everyone has completed this survey, the forms will be collected and reviewed by your teacher. Your teacher will not know who completed each individual survey.

Table 2.2. K-5 Classroom Management Survey

Statement	Strongly Agree	Agree	Disagree	Strongly Disagree
I understand the classroom rules.				
I understand the reasons why we have these rules.				
My teacher recognizes students that follow the rules.				
My teacher applies classroom rules fairly.				
My teacher cares about me as a person.				
My teacher expects all students to participate.				
My teacher knows when students misbehave.				
My teacher is in charge of this classroom.				
My teacher remains calm when a student misbehaves.				
I need to work hard to succeed in this class.				
With my teacher's help, I can learn things that are difficult.				

STUDENT SURVEY—SECONDARY VERSION
CLASSROOM MANAGEMENT

Date: _____ Class Period: _____

Directions: Please read the statements below. For each statement place an X in the box that identifies your level of agreement with that statement. **Do not write your name on this survey**. When everyone has completed this survey, the forms will be collected and reviewed by your teacher. Your teacher will not know who completed each individual survey.

Table 2.3. 6-12 Classroom Management Survey

Statement	Strongly Agree	Agree	Disagree	Strongly Disagree
I understand the expectations and procedures in this classroom.				
I understand the reasons for why we have these expectations and procedures.				
My teacher recognizes students that follow the rules and procedures.				
My teacher applies classroom expectations fairly.				
My teacher cares about me as more than just a student.				
My teacher expects everyone to participate.				
My teacher is aware of the behavior of all of the students in the classroom.				
My teacher has control of this classroom.				
My teacher does not hold grudges or take misbehavior personally.				
Effort is necessary for success in this classroom.				
If I try different approaches and persist when faced with challenging work, I can eventually succeed.				

STUDENT SURVEY SUMMARY (FORM 1)

Teacher's Name: _____ School Year: _____

Grade: _____ Subject: _____

Survey Version Given: _____ Elementary _____ Secondary

Student Response Analysis

1. Describe the grade level, subject area, and number of students:

2. List any factors that might have influenced the responses:

3. What did students perceive as your strengths?

4. What did students perceive as your weaknesses?

5. What, if anything, do you need to do differently as a result of these responses?

STUDENT SURVEY SUMMARY (FORM 2)

Teacher's Name: _____ School Year: _____

Grade: _____ Subject: _____

Survey Version Given: _____ Elementary _____ Secondary

Student Response Analysis

1. List any factors that might have influenced the responses:

2. What did students perceive as your strengths?

3. What did students perceive as your weaknesses?

4. What, if anything, changed significantly since the first time you administered the student survey?

TEACHER VIDEO REFLECTION (FORM 1)

Teacher's Name: _____ School Year: _____

Grade: _____ Subject: _____

The area of my classroom management that I have targeted for analysis is:

After reviewing the videotaped segment, I rate my use of this area of classroom management as:

Table 2.4. Performance Rating Scale

Proficient	Developing	Beginning

The evidence for this rating from the video is:

Table 2.5. Evidence for Rating

TEACHER EVIDENCE	STUDENT EVIDENCE

TEACHER VIDEO REFLECTION (FORM 2)

Teacher's Name: _____ School Year: _____

Grade: _____ Subject: _____

The area of my classroom management that I have targeted for analysis is:

After reviewing the videotaped segment, I rate my use of this area of classroom management as:

Table 2.6. Performance Rating Scale

Proficient	Developing	Beginning

The evidence for this rating from the video is:

Table 2.7. Evidence for Rating

TEACHER EVIDENCE	STUDENT EVIDENCE

PORTFOLIO—YEAR ONE CLASSROOM MANAGEMENT

This portfolio is a collection of your work. It represents you and the work that you have done during this school year. Some of the work will need to be selected, while other work will need to be created for this portfolio. For work which you select, staple on top a cover sheet that explains to the reader **what the selection is, what you thought of it, what you learned from it**, and anything else you would like to include. Each cover sheet must be between one and three paragraphs.

1. **COVER LETTER**: Give the reader an introduction to you and your portfolio. Include **one separate paragraph** for each of the following:
   a. Describe the rationale for how you have organized your classroom. Specifically, articulate why you made the choices you have made.
   b. Describe the process used to identify, teach, and reinforce classroom rules and routines.
   c. Describe the strategies used to display an appropriate balance between cooperation and assertiveness with students.
   d. Describe the strategies used to maintain emotional objectivity with regard to student misbehavior.
   e. Describe the strategies used to encourage students to persist when confronted with challenging academic tasks.
2. **REQUIRED ELEMENTS**:
   a. Student Survey Summary Forms 1 and 2
   b. Teacher Video Reflection Forms 1 and 2
3. **CHOICES**: (Be sure to include a cover sheet for each choice.)
   a. Choose an artifact that demonstrates *something you did well* in the domain of classroom management.
   b. Choose an artifact that demonstrates *something you need to improve* in the domain of classroom management.
   c. Choose an artifact that demonstrates *your growth over the course of the year* in the domain of classroom management.
4. **PRESENTATION**:
   a. Include a table of contents and make sure your work is submitted in order.

(Staple to inside front cover of manila folder.)

Table 2.8. Portfolio Assessment Form

PORTFOLIO ASSESSMENT FORM				
	SCORE 3.0	SCORE 2.0	SCORE 1.0	SCORE 0
COVER LETTER	Five separate paragraphs each of which meets **all** of the specified requirements.	Five separate paragraphs, each of which meets **most** of the specified requirements.	Five separate paragraphs, each of which meets **some** of the specified requirements.	No cover letter included or missing entire required sections.
REQUIRED ELEMENTS	All of the elements required are submitted. The reflection for each item is thoughtful and comprehensive.	All of the elements required are submitted, however at least some aspects of the reflections are superficial.	Some of the required elements are submitted.	None of the required elements are submitted.
CHOICES	Three items selected, each of which has a cover sheet that meets **all** of the specified requirements.	Three items selected, each of which has a cover sheet that meets **most** of the specified requirements.	Three items selected, each of which has a cover sheet that meets **some** of the specified requirements.	Missing one or more of the required choices.

TOTAL SCORE: _____ /9

(Staple to inside rear cover of manila folder.)

CLASSROOM MANAGEMENT TEACHER OBSERVATION FORM

Date: _____ Time: _____

Teacher's Name: _____ Observer: _____

Table 2.9. Classroom Management Rating Domains

EVIDENCE	OBSERVED	NOT OBSERVED	N/A
PHYSICAL ORGANIZATION OF CLASSROOM			
The physical layout of the classroom has clear traffic patterns.			
The physical layout of the classroom provides easy access to materials.			
The classroom is decorated in a way that enhances student learning.			
Bulletin boards relate to relevant content.			
Student work is displayed.			
Daily schedule is posted.			
Comments:			
CLASSROOM RULES AND PROCEDURES			
Rules are visible for students.			
Rules are stated positively and in behavioral terms.			
Rules are doable and manageable.			

EVIDENCE	OBSERVED	NOT OBSERVED	N/A
Procedures are developed for common classroom activities.			
Students are able to independently follow classroom procedures.			
Comments:			
REINFORCING CLASSROOM EXPECTATIONS			
Teacher uses nonverbal signals to communicate that behavior is either appropriate or inappropriate.			
Teacher uses verbal statements to communicate that behavior is either appropriate or inappropriate.			
Teacher uses direct consequences when necessary.			
Teacher uses intervention strategies that are at the lowest level of "intrusiveness."			
Teacher provides feedback on behavior that is specific and descriptive.			
Students cease inappropriate behavior when the teacher uses verbal or nonverbal signals.			
Teacher provides students with positive statements far more frequently than negative statements.			

(continued)

Table 2.9. (continued)

EVIDENCE	OBSERVED	NOT OBSERVED	N/A
Comments:			
TEACHER-STUDENT RELATIONSHIPS			
Teacher compliments students regarding academic and/or personal accomplishments.			
At the appropriate time, the teacher engages in informal conversations with students that are not academic.			
Teacher uses humor appropriately.			
Teacher frequently smiles and nods at students.			
Comments:			
MENTAL SET			
Teacher maintains a calm and controlled demeanor.			
Teacher scans the entire classroom, making eye contact with all students.			

EVIDENCE	OBSERVED	NOT OBSERVED	N/A
Teacher remains able to see all of the actions of the students in the classroom.			

Comments:

REINFORCING EFFORT			
Teacher provides feedback that emphasizes the value of planning and trying different approaches.			
Teacher encourages students to see learning challenges as opportunities to improve skills and understanding.			
Teacher uses and encourages students to use the word "yet" to change discouraging statements into positive ones.			

Comments:

Date of Post-Conference: _____

Signature of Observer: _____ Date: _____

Signature of Teacher: _____ Date: _____

TEACHER SUMMATIVE EVALUATION REPORT

Teacher: _____ Academic Year: _____

Table 2.10. Classroom Management and Professionalism Rubrics

DOMAIN 1—CLASSROOM MANAGEMENT			
SUBDOMAIN	PROFICIENT	DEVELOPING	BEGINNING
Physical Organization of Classroom	Effectively organizes the classroom to facilitate movement and promote a focus on learning.	Some of the aspects of the physical organization of the classroom facilitate movement and promote a focus on learning.	The organization of the classroom does not facilitate movement, nor does it promote a focus on learning.
Establishment of Classroom Rules and Procedures	Effectively develops expectations and procedures to encourage positive student behavior.	Aspects of the expectations and procedures are effective, but other aspects are missing or ineffective.	The expectations and procedures for encouraging positive student behavior are neither comprehensive nor effective.
Reinforcement of Expectations	**Consistently** and **effectively** both acknowledges and reinforces positive student behavior and provides appropriate consequences for undesirable student behavior.	**Occasionally** acknowledges and reinforces positive student behavior and provides appropriate consequences for undesirable student behavior.	Neither acknowledges and reinforces positive student behavior nor provides appropriate consequences for undesirable student behavior.

SUBDOMAIN	PROFICIENT	DEVELOPING	BEGINNING
Teacher-Student Relationships	**Consistently** and **effectively** uses verbal and nonverbal behaviors to develop and maintain positive relationships with students.	**Occasionally** uses verbal and nonverbal behaviors to develop and maintain positive relationships with students.	**Does not** consistently use verbal and nonverbal behaviors to develop and maintain positive relationships with students.
Mental Set	**Consistently** and **effectively** both demonstrates awareness of the actions of all of the students in the classroom and behaves in a manner that is objective and controlled.	**Occasionally** demonstrates awareness of the actions of all of the students in the classroom. Usually behaves in a manner that is objective and controlled.	Neither demonstrates awareness of the actions of all of the students in the classroom nor behaves in a manner that is objective and controlled.
Reinforcement of Effort	**Consistently** and **effectively** both uses explicit strategies to foster the understanding of the relationship between effort and achievement, and acknowledges students' efforts when they work hard to achieve.	**Occasionally** uses explicit strategies to foster the understanding of the relationship between effort and achievement, and acknowledges students' efforts when they work hard to achieve.	Neither uses explicit strategies to foster the understanding of the relationship between effort and achievement, nor acknowledges students' efforts when they work hard to achieve.
Comments:			

(continued)

Table 2.10. (continued)

DOMAIN 4—PROFESSIONALISM			
SUBDOMAIN	PROFICIENT	DEVELOPING	BEGINNING
Respect for Others	**Consistently** demonstrates respect for every member of the organization.	There have been **isolated incidents** of not demonstrating respect for others.	**Frequently does not** demonstrate respect for every member of the organization.
Dependability	**Consistently** follows through on assigned tasks and completes promised actions in a timely manner.	There have been **isolated incidents** of not demonstrating dependability.	Neither follows through on assigned tasks, nor completes promised actions in a timely manner.
Honesty	**Consistently** tells the truth with the appropriate degree of tact.	There have been **isolated incidents** of not demonstrating honesty.	**Frequently does not** tell the truth with the appropriate degree of tact.
Accountability	**Consistently** accepts responsibility for achieving meaningful student growth over time.	There have been **isolated incidents** of not demonstrating accountability.	**Frequently does not** accept responsibility for achieving meaningful student growth over time.
Integrity	**Consistently** expresses beliefs appropriately, and models the ability to do what they believe is right in the face of challenging circumstances.	There have been **isolated incidents** of not demonstrating integrity.	Neither expresses their beliefs appropriately, nor models the ability to do what they believe is right in the face of challenging circumstances.

SUBDOMAIN	PROFICIENT	DEVELOPING	BEGINNING
Risk-Taking	**Consistently** demonstrates willingness to try new strategies, as well as takes the initiative to learn from attempts that did not achieve desired results.	There have been **isolated incidents** of not demonstrating risk-taking.	Neither demonstrates willingness to try new strategies nor takes the initiative to learn from attempts that did not achieve desired results.
Humility	**Consistently** considers the needs and feelings of others, accepts constructive criticism, and asks for assistance when necessary.	There have been **isolated incidents** of not demonstrating humility.	Neither considers the needs and feelings of others, nor accepts constructive criticism. Does not seek assistance when necessary.
Collaboration	**Consistently** collaborates with colleagues in a genuine manner.	There have been **isolated incidents** of not demonstrating collaboration.	**Frequently does not** collaborate with colleagues in a genuine manner.
Comments:			

Teacher's Signature:_____ Date:_____

Evaluator's Signature:_____ Date:_____

3

Year Two: Direct Instruction and Professionalism

OVERVIEW OF YEAR TWO

Welcome to year two of our district's teacher induction program. The goal for this year will be for you to demonstrate proficiency in the area of instruction and continued proficiency in the areas of classroom management and professionalism. More specifically, it is expected that you will demonstrate proficient implementation of the following district teaching standards. The teacher effectively and consistently:

- uses prime-times for learning.
- uses physical movement activities to maintain student engagement.
- paces the presentation of content and demonstrates enthusiasm for the content presented.
- creates and communicates student learning objectives.
- uses strategies to facilitate student understanding of the importance of learning the content.
- uses strategies to engage students in an anticipatory set.
- uses a variety of strategies to provide the content necessary for students to achieve the objective.
- uses models and examples to accurately and clearly highlight the critical attributes of new content.
- uses a variety of methods to verify students' understanding of the content presented.
- provides students with guided practice opportunities.
- provides students with the opportunity to achieve closure of what has been learned.
- provides students with independent practice activities.

Of course, other aspects of teaching such as assessment remain important. However, these will not serve as the focus for professional growth and evaluation in your second year.

In order to assist you in meeting these goals, you will participate in a collegial study of the second section of the book *From First Year to First Rate: Thriving during the Initial Years of Your Teaching Career* (Jennings, 2021). While reading the assigned section of the text you will be expected to make annotations. This will help you prepare for each study session. In these sessions, you will participate with colleagues in the discussion of questions designed to build understanding of the content.

Additionally, you will have opportunities to obtain student perception of your work through collection and reflection on student surveys. Another opportunity for reflection will be through self-analysis of videotaped segments of your classroom performance. The student surveys, reflections of video, and other required items will be assembled into a teacher portfolio that will be provided to your lead observer.

You will have multiple classroom observations throughout the course of the school year. These observations will focus on your implementation of the previously listed standards. As these observations are intended to be formative, they will not provide you with performance ratings. Instead, you will receive constructive feedback on your implementation of the standards.

The content of your portfolio and formal and informal observations by your supervisor(s) will be combined with other relevant data to draw conclusions related to your progress. At a summative conference you will receive final ratings of your performance toward these standards. These ratings will be used to make decisions regarding additional professional development opportunities as well as continued employment in the school district.

The goal of the school district is to see you succeed. It will require effort on your part, but you will receive abundant support throughout the process. At the conclusion of this year, it is our sincere desire to see that you have established proficiency with these standards so that you are prepared to progress to the next phase of our induction program.

TASK-SPECIFIC DIRECTIONS AND TIMELINES

Student Survey Administration

1. You shall administer the appropriate student survey. Grades K–5 will use the elementary version and grades 6–12 will complete the secondary version. If the students are not able to read the survey independently, you may read the statements aloud, allowing students to respond to each in turn.
2. If multiple classes composed of different students are taught, choose one class to survey. This shall be the same class for both survey administrations.
3. Administration of surveys shall occur twice, according to the deadlines provided. After the survey has been completed, you are to compile the results and complete the required self-reflection form. The surveys themselves remain the property of the teacher.
4. The required self-reflection forms shall be included in your portfolio.

Video Self-Analysis

1. Using a personal or district-owned recording device, you are required to record and reflect upon two lessons throughout the course of the school year. Deadlines for completing this task are provided.
2. The length of the recorded video shall be a minimum of twenty minutes. During year two, the focus of your analysis shall be on the implementation of instructional strategies.
3. You are to watch the video and complete the required self-reflection form.
4. The self-reflection forms are required elements of the teacher portfolio.

Teacher Portfolio

1. You are required to submit a portfolio that contains the following elements:
    a. Reflective writing focused on the corresponding goals of the year.

b. Required elements:
   i. Student Survey Summary Forms 1 and 2
   ii. Teacher Video Reflection Forms 1 and 2
c. Three choice items selected by the teacher. Different choices are required for each year.
2. This portfolio must be submitted to the teacher's evaluator by the date specified on the list of deadlines below.
3. The goal of this portfolio is to be concise and reflective. You may not add additional elements, nor is there any value in going beyond the requirements listed.
4. You will receive feedback on the quality of this portfolio during your summative evaluation conference.

Summative Ratings

1. Your final evaluation will be based upon scores for rubrics aligned to each standard that serves as the focus for the year. In addition, you will receive scores for your level of proficiency in classroom management and professionalism standards. The rubrics are included for your review.
2. Your evaluator will use observational data and the contents of your portfolio to make a summative judgment of your performance. This summative judgment will be used to decisions regarding renewal of employment and may lead to additional professional development opportunities.

CLASSROOM INSTRUCTION RUBRIC

Teacher's Signature:_____ Date:_____

Evaluator's Signature:_____ Date:_____

Table 3.1. Classroom Instruction Rubrics

SUBDOMAIN	EFFECTIVE	PARTIALLY EFFECTIVE	INEFFECTIVE
Instructional Prime-Times	The teacher **consistently and effectively** uses prime-times for learning.	The teacher attempts to use prime-times for learning but is only **partially successful**.	The teacher **does not** consistently and effectively use prime-times for learning.
Physical Movement	The teacher **consistently and effectively** uses physical movement activities.	The teacher attempts to use physical movement activities but is only **partially successful**.	The teacher **does not** consistently and effectively use physical movement activities.
Presentation Skills	The teacher **consistently and effectively** uses pacing and demonstrates enthusiasm for the content being presented.	The teacher attempts to use pacing and demonstrate enthusiasm for the content being presented but is only **partially successful**.	The teacher **does not** consistently and effectively use effective pacing and/or **does not** demonstrate enthusiasm for the content being presented.
Learning Objectives	The teacher **consistently and effectively** creates and communicates learning objectives.	The teacher attempts to create and communicate learning objectives but is only **partially successful**.	The teacher **does not** consistently and effectively create and communicate learning objectives.

(continued)

Table 3.1. (continued)

SUBDOMAIN	EFFECTIVE	PARTIALLY EFFECTIVE	INEFFECTIVE
Purpose	The teacher **consistently and effectively** uses strategies to help students see the reason for learning content.	The teacher attempts to use strategies to help students see the reason for learning the content but is only **partially successful**.	The teacher **does not** consistently and effectively use strategies to help students see the reason for learning content.
Anticipatory Set	The teacher **consistently and effectively** uses an anticipatory set to focus students' attention on content to be learned and activate relevant prior knowledge.	The teacher attempts to use an anticipatory set to focus students' attention on content to be learned and activate relevant prior knowledge but is only **partially successful**.	The teacher **does not** consistently and effectively use an anticipatory set to focus students' attention on content to be learned and activate relevant prior knowledge.
Input	The teacher **consistently and effectively** uses a variety of strategies to provide the information necessary for students to achieve the objective.	The teacher attempts to use a variety of strategies to provide the information necessary for students to achieve the objective but is only **partially successful**.	The teacher **does not** consistently and effectively use a variety of strategies to provide the information necessary for students to achieve the objective.
Models/ Examples	The teacher **consistently and effectively** uses models and examples.	The teacher attempts to use models and examples but is only **partially successful**.	The teacher **does not** consistently and effectively use models and examples.

SUBDOMAIN	EFFECTIVE	PARTIALLY EFFECTIVE	INEFFECTIVE
Checking for Understanding	The teacher **consistently and effectively** uses a variety of methods to verify students' understanding.	The teacher attempts to use a variety of methods to verify students' understanding but is only **partially successful**.	The teacher **does not** consistently and effectively use a variety of methods to verify students' understanding.
Guided Practice	The teacher **consistently and effectively** provides massed and distributed practice opportunities.	The teacher attempts to provide massed and distributed practice opportunities but is only **partially successful**.	The teacher **does not** consistently and effectively provide massed and distributed practice opportunities.
Closure	The teacher **consistently and effectively** provides students with the opportunities to summarize for themself their perception of what has been learned.	The teacher attempts to provide students with opportunities to summarize for him or herself their perception of what has been learned but is only **partially successful**.	The teacher **does not** consistently and effectively provide students with the opportunities to summarize for him or herself their perception of what has been learned.
Independent Practice	The teacher **consistently and effectively** provides learners with independent practice activities.	The teacher attempts to provide learners with independent practice activities but is only **partially successful**.	The teacher **does not** consistently and effectively provide learner(s) with independent practice activities.

Chapter 3

DEADLINES FOR TASK COMPLETION

Book Study Group Meeting #1: Date: _____ Time: _____
Location: _____
Book Study Group Meeting #2: Date: _____ Time: _____
Location: _____
Book Study Group Meeting #3: Date: _____ Time: _____
Location: _____
Video Analysis #1: Date: _____ Video Analysis #2: Date: _____
Student Survey #1: Date: _____ Student Survey #2: Date: _____
Portfolio Due Date: _____

STUDENT SURVEY—ELEMENTARY VERSION
CLASSROOM INSTRUCTION

Date: _____ Class Period: _____

Directions: Please read the statements below. For each statement place an X in the box that identifies how much you agree with that statement. **Do not write your name on this survey.** When everyone has completed this survey, the forms will be collected and reviewed by your teacher. Your teacher will not know who completed each individual survey.

Table 3.2. K-5 Student Survey

Statement	Strongly Agree	Agree	Disagree	Strongly Disagree
I am able to pay attention to my teacher's presentations.				
The pace of this class is good for me.				
My teacher likes the subject(s) he or she teaches.				
My teacher enjoys teaching.				
I know what I am supposed to learn.				
I know when I am successful in learning the content.				
I know why it is important to learn the content my teacher teaches.				
I know how what we are learning connects to things we have already learned.				
How my teacher presents information helps me learn it.				
When my teacher asks questions, he or she gives me enough time to come up with an answer.				
My teacher gives me enough time to practice what we learn.				
I understand the reason for the homework assignments I am told to complete.				
I am able to complete my homework assignments on my own.				

STUDENT SURVEY—SECONDARY VERSION
CLASSROOM INSTRUCTION

Date: _____ Class Period: _____

Directions: Please read the statements below. For each statement place an X in the box that identifies your level of agreement with that statement. **Do not write your name on this survey**. When everyone has completed this survey, the forms will be collected and reviewed by your teacher. Your teacher will not know who completed each individual survey.

Table 3.3. 6-12 Student Survey

Statement	Strongly Agree	Agree	Disagree	Strongly Disagree
I am able to maintain focused attention on teacher presentations.				
The pace of this class is good for me.				
My teacher likes the content he or she teaches.				
My teacher enjoys teaching.				
I know what I am expected to learn.				
I know when I am successful in learning the content.				
I know the reason why it is important to learn the content.				
I know how the content we learn connects to other things we have learned.				
The way the teacher presents information helps me to learn it.				
When my teacher asks questions, he or she gives me enough time to come up with an answer.				
My teacher gives me enough time to practice what we learn.				
I understand the reason for the homework assignments I am told to complete.				
I am able to independently complete my homework assignments.				

STUDENT SURVEY SUMMARY (FORM 1)

Teacher's Name: _____ School Year: _____

Grade: _____ Subject: _____

Survey Version Given: _____ Elementary _____ Secondary

Student Response Analysis

1. Describe the grade level, subject area, and number of students:

2. List any factors that might have influenced the responses:

3. What did students perceive as your strengths?

4. What did students perceive as your weaknesses?

5. What, if anything, do you need to do differently as a result of these responses?

STUDENT SURVEY SUMMARY (FORM 2)

Teacher's Name: _____ School Year: _____

Grade: _____ Subject: _____

Survey Version Given: _____ Elementary _____ Secondary

Student Response Analysis

1. List any factors that might have influenced the responses:

2. What did students perceive as your strengths?

3. What did students perceive as your weaknesses?

4. What, if anything, changed significantly since the first time you administered the student survey?

TEACHER VIDEO REFLECTION (FORM 1)

Teacher's Name: _____ School Year: _____

Grade: _____ Subject: _____

The area of my classroom management that I have targeted for analysis is:

After reviewing the videotaped segment, I rate my use of this area of classroom management as:

Table 3.4. Proficiency Rating Scale

Proficient	Developing	Beginning

The evidence for this rating from the video is:

Table 3.5. Evidence for Rating

TEACHER EVIDENCE	STUDENT EVIDENCE

TEACHER VIDEO REFLECTION (FORM 2)

Teacher's Name: _____ School Year: _____

Grade: _____ Subject: _____

The area of my classroom management that I have targeted for analysis is:

After reviewing the videotaped segment, I rate my use of this area of classroom management as:

Table 3.6. Proficiency Rating Scale

Proficient	Developing	Beginning

The evidence for this rating from the video is:

Table 3.7. Evidence for Rating

TEACHER EVIDENCE	STUDENT EVIDENCE

PORTFOLIO—YEAR TWO CLASSROOM INSTRUCTION

This portfolio is a collection of your work. It represents you and the work that you have done during this school year. Some of the work will need to be selected, while other work will need to be created for this portfolio. For work which you select, staple on top a cover sheet that explains to the reader **what the selection is**, **what you thought of it**, **what you learned from it**, and anything else you would like to include. Each cover sheet must be between one and three paragraphs.

1. **COVER LETTER**: Give the reader an introduction to you and your portfolio. Include **one separate paragraph** for each of the following:
   a. Describe the process you use to plan instruction.
   b. Describe how you demonstrate enthusiasm for the content you teach.
   c. Describe how you have incorporated distributed practice of prior learning.
   d. Describe how you have changed your questioning practices over the course of this school year.
2. **REQUIRED ELEMENTS:**
   a. Student Survey Summary Forms 1 and 2
   b. Teacher Video Reflection Forms 1 and 2
3. **CHOICES** (Be sure to include a cover sheet for each choice.)
   a. Choose a lesson plan that demonstrates knowledge of all of the elements of direct instruction.
   b. Choose an example of how you established the relevance of the content with students.
   c. Choose an example of a successful closure activity.
4. **PRESENTATION**:
   a. Include a table of contents and make sure your work is submitted in order.

   (Staple to inside front cover of manila folder.)

Table 3.8. Portfolio Assessment Form

PORTFOLIO ASSESSMENT FORM				
	SCORE 3.0	SCORE 2.0	SCORE 1.0	SCORE 0
COVER LETTER	Five separate paragraphs each of which meets **all** of the specified requirements.	Five separate paragraphs, each of which meets **most** of the specified requirements.	Five separate paragraphs, each of which meets **some** of the specified requirements.	No cover letter included or missing entire required sections.
REQUIRED ELEMENTS	All of the elements required are submitted. The reflection for each item is thoughtful and comprehensive.	All of the elements required are submitted, however at least some aspects of the reflections are superficial.	Some of the required elements are submitted.	None of the required elements are submitted.
CHOICES	Three items selected, each of which has a cover sheet that meets **all** of the specified requirements.	Three items selected, each of which has a cover sheet that meets **most** of the specified requirements.	Three items selected, each of which has a cover sheet that meets **some** of the specified requirements.	Missing one or more of the required choices.

TOTAL SCORE: _____ /9

(Staple to inside rear cover of manila folder.)

CLASSROOM INSTRUCTION TEACHER OBSERVATION FORM

Date: _____ Time: _____

Teacher's Name: _____ Observer: _____

Table 3.9. Observations of Instruction

EVIDENCE	OBSERVED	NOT OBSERVED	N/A
USE OF PRIME INSTRUCTIONAL TIME			
Upon gaining student attention, the teacher presents accurate, new information.			
Teacher provides opportunity for closure during Prime-Time 2.			
Teacher uses down-time for review and practice.			
Teacher provides multiple learning segments by incorporating "structured breaks".			
Students are able to sustain focused attention on the teacher's presentation.			
PHYSICAL MOVEMENT			
Teacher has students do physical activities to increase energy levels.			
Students engage in physical activities designed by teacher.			
PRESENTATION SKILLS			
Teacher employs effective transitions from one activity to the next.			
Teacher alters pace as necessary.			
Teacher describes personal experiences related to the content.			
Teacher uses physical gestures, voice tone, or dramatization of information to signal enthusiasm for content.			

(continued)

Table 3.9. (*continued*)

EVIDENCE	OBSERVED	NOT OBSERVED	N/A
Teacher uses multisensory activities.			
Students quickly adapt to transitions and reengage when an activity begins.			
LEARNING OBJECTIVES			
Differences in essential content presented far outweigh similarities.			
Objective is written in student-friendly language and is visible for students to see.			
PURPOSE			
The teacher explains the importance of learning the content.			
The teacher's explanation is likely to be meaningful to the majority of students.			
ANTICIPATORY SET			
Teacher uses activities to determine what students already know about the topic.			
Teacher uses activities to focus student attention on the most important content to be learned.			
Teacher uses information provided by students to make instructional decisions.			
INPUT			
Teacher provides the input students require for performing the skill or demonstrating the knowledge in the content of the learning objective.			

EVIDENCE	OBSERVED	NOT OBSERVED	N/A
Teacher clearly articulates what makes the content different from all other similar concepts.			
Teacher uses a sensible organizational pattern to present the information.			
Teacher presents the information both verbally and visually.			
Teacher uses strategies to emphasize critical information.			
Teacher provides students with active processing opportunities after each "chunk" of critical content.			
Teacher requires students to record and represent new, critical content.			
MODELS/EXAMPLES			
Teacher provides appropriate models and examples.			
The models/examples provided are both accurate and identify the critical attributes of the new learning.			
The teacher avoids controversial issues and non-examples when introducing the new content.			
CHECKING FOR UNDERSTANDING			
When asking questions, teacher provides students with a minimum of three seconds of think-time.			
When selecting students to provide an answer to a question, the teacher predominantly uses random selection methods.			

(continued)

Table 3.9. (*continued*)

EVIDENCE	OBSERVED	NOT OBSERVED	N/A
Additional think-time is provided after students provide a correct answer.			
The teacher persists with students who do not get the correct answer.			
The teacher uses whole-group participation strategies to increase the active involvement of all students.			
GUIDED PRACTICE			
Practice periods are short and focused.			
Teacher provides prompt, specific corrective feedback to students.			
Students are engaged and focused on completing practice activities.			
Students voluntarily ask clarification questions and seek help when needed.			
CLOSURE			
Teacher provides specific directions for what the learner should process.			
Teacher provides a clear description of the overt product required.			
Time provided for closure activity is sufficient.			
INDEPENDENT PRACTICE			
The teacher communicates a clear purpose for the independent practice activities assigned.			

Date of Post-Conference: _____

Signature of Observer: _____ Date: _____

Signature of Teacher: _____ Date: _____

TEACHER SUMMATIVE EVALUATION REPORT

Teacher: _____ Academic Year: _____

Table 3.10. Instruction Performance Rubric Ratings

SUBDOMAIN	EFFECTIVE	PARTIALLY EFFECTIVE	INEFFECTIVE
Instructional Prime-Times	The teacher **consistently and effectively** uses prime-times for learning.	The teacher attempts to use prime-times for learning but is only **partially successful**.	The teacher **does not** consistently and effectively use prime-times for learning.
Physical Movement	The teacher **consistently and effectively** uses physical movement activities.	The teacher attempts to use physical movement activities but is only **partially successful**.	The teacher **does not** consistently and effectively use physical movement activities.
Presentation Skills	The teacher **consistently and effectively** uses pacing and demonstrates enthusiasm for the content being presented.	The teacher attempts to use pacing and demonstrate enthusiasm for the content being presented but is only **partially successful**.	The teacher **does not** consistently and effectively use effective pacing and/or does not demonstrate enthusiasm for the content being presented.
Learning Objectives	The teacher **consistently and effectively** creates and communicates learning objectives.	The teacher attempts to create and communicate learning objectives but is only partially successful.	The teacher **does not** consistently and effectively create and communicate learning objectives.
Purpose	The teacher **consistently and effectively** uses strategies to help students see the reason for learning content.	The teacher attempts to use strategies to help students see the reason for learning the content but is only **partially successful**.	The teacher **does not** consistently and effectively use strategies to help students see the reason for learning content.

(continued)

Table 3.10. *(continued)*

SUBDOMAIN	EFFECTIVE	PARTIALLY EFFECTIVE	INEFFECTIVE
Anticipatory Set	The teacher **consistently and effectively** uses an anticipatory set to focus students' attention on content to be learned and activate relevant prior knowledge.	The teacher attempts to use an anticipatory set to focus students' attention on content to be learned and activate relevant prior knowledge but is only **partially successful**.	The teacher **does not** consistently and effectively use an anticipatory set to focus students' attention on content to be learned and activate relevant prior knowledge.
Input	The teacher **consistently and effectively** uses a variety of strategies to provide the information necessary for students to achieve the objective.	The teacher attempts to use a variety of strategies to provide the information necessary for students to achieve the objective but is only **partially successful**.	The teacher does not consistently and effectively use a variety of strategies to provide the information necessary for students to achieve the objective.
Models/ Examples	The teacher **consistently and effectively** uses models and examples.	The teacher attempts to use models and examples but is only **partially successful**.	The teacher **does not** consistently and effectively use models and examples.
Checking for Understanding	The teacher **consistently and effectively** uses a variety of methods to verify students' understanding.	The teacher attempts to use a variety of methods to verify students' understanding but is only **partially successful**.	The teacher **does not** consistently and effectively use a variety of methods to verify students' understanding.
Guided Practice	The teacher **consistently and effectively** provides massed and distributed practice opportunities.	The teacher attempts to provide massed and distributed practice opportunities but is only **partially successful**.	The teacher **does not** consistently and effectively provide massed and distributed practice opportunities.

SUBDOMAIN	EFFECTIVE	PARTIALLY EFFECTIVE	INEFFECTIVE
Closure	The teacher **consistently and effectively** provides students with the opportunities to summarize for themself their perception of what has been learned.	The teacher attempts to provide students with opportunities to summarize for him or herself their perception of what has been learned but is only **partially successful**.	The teacher **does not** consistently and effectively provide students with the opportunities to summarize for him or herself their perception of what has been learned.
Independent Practice	The teacher **consistently and effectively** provides learners with independent practice activities.	The teacher attempts to provide learners with independent practice activities but is only **partially successful**.	The teacher **does not** consistently and effectively provide learner(s) with independent practice activities.
PREVIOUS DOMAINS		**PERFORMANCE RATING**	
DOMAIN 1—Classroom Management		Continues to meet expectations	Does not continue to meet expectations
DOMAIN 4—Professionalism		Continues to meet expectations	Does not continue to meet expectations

Teacher's Signature: _____ Date: _____

Evaluator's Signature: _____ Date: _____

4

Year Three: Classroom Assessment and Professionalism

OVERVIEW OF YEAR THREE

Welcome to year three of our district's teacher induction program. The goal for this year will be for you to demonstrate proficiency in the area of assessment and continued proficiency in the areas of classroom management, instruction, and professionalism. More specifically, it is expected that you will demonstrate proficient implementation of the following district teaching standards. The teacher effectively and consistently:

- provides students with high quality feedback on performance.
- uses research-based strategies to gather accurate information about student achievement.
- uses assessment results to make data-driven decisions targeted towards improving student achievement.

In order to assist you in meeting these goals, you will participate in a collegial study of the third section of the book *From First Year to First Rate: Thriving during the Initial Years of Your Teaching Career* (Jennings, 2021). While reading the assigned section of the text you will be expected to make annotations. This will help you prepare for each study session. In these sessions, you will participate with colleagues in the discussion of questions designed to build understanding of the content.

Additionally, you will have opportunities to obtain student perception of your work through collection and reflection on student surveys.

The student surveys and other required items will be assembled into a teacher portfolio that will be provided to your lead observer.

You will have multiple classroom observations throughout the course of the school year. These observations will focus on your implementation of previously addressed standards. As these observations are intended to be formative, they will not provide you with performance ratings. Instead, you will receive constructive feedback on your implementation of the standards.

The content of your portfolio and formal and informal observations by your supervisor(s) will be combined with other relevant data to draw conclusions related to your progress. At a summative conference you will receive final ratings of your performance toward these standards. These ratings will be used to make decisions regarding additional professional development opportunities as well as continued employment in the school district.

The goal of the school district is to see you succeed. It will require effort on your part, but you will receive abundant support throughout the process. At the conclusion of this year, it is our sincere desire to see that you have established proficiency with these standards so that you are prepared to progress to the next phase of our professional development program.

TASK-SPECIFIC DIRECTIONS AND TIMELINES

Student Survey Administration

1. You shall administer the appropriate student survey. Grades K–5 will use the elementary version and grades 6–12 will complete the secondary version. If the students are not able to read the survey independently, you may read the statements aloud, allowing students to respond to each in turn.
2. If multiple classes composed of different students are taught, choose one class to survey. This shall be the same class for both survey administrations.
3. Administration of surveys shall occur twice, according to the deadlines provided. After the survey has been completed, you are

to compile the results and complete the required self-reflection form. The surveys themselves remain the property of the teacher.
4. The required self-reflection forms shall be included in your portfolio.

Teacher Portfolio

1. You are required to submit a portfolio that contains the following elements:
   a. Reflective writing focused on the corresponding goals of the year.
   b. Required elements:
      i. Student Survey Summary Forms 1 and 2
   c. Three choice items selected by the teacher. Different choices are required for each year.
2. This portfolio must be submitted to the teacher's evaluator by the date specified on the list of deadlines below.
3. The goal of this portfolio is to be concise and reflective. You may not add additional elements, nor is there any value in going beyond the requirements listed.
4. You will receive feedback on the quality of this portfolio during your summative evaluation conference.

Summative Ratings

1. Your final evaluation will be based upon scores for rubrics aligned to each standard that serves as the focus for the year. In addition, you will receive scores for your level of proficiency in classroom management, instruction, and professionalism standards. The rubrics are included for your review.
2. Your evaluator will use observational data and the contents of your documentation log to make a summative judgment of your performance. This summative judgment will be used to decisions regarding renewal of employment and may lead to additional professional development opportunities.

CLASSROOM ASSESSMENT SUMMATIVE EVALUATION

Table 4.1. Classroom Assessment Performance Rating Rubrics

SUBDOMAIN	PROFICIENT	DEVELOPING	BEGINNING
Feedback	The teacher **consistently and effectively** provides students with high-quality feedback on performance.	The teacher attempts to provide students with high-quality feedback but is only **partially successful**.	The teacher **does not** consistently and effectively provide students with high-quality feedback.
Assessment Strategies	The teacher **consistently and effectively** uses research-based strategies to gather accurate information about student achievement.	The teacher attempts to use research-based strategies to gather accurate information about student achievement but is only **partially successful**.	The teacher **does not** consistently and effectively use research-based strategies to gather accurate information about student achievement.
Data Use	The teacher **consistently and effectively** uses assessment results to make data-driven decisions targeted toward improving student achievement.	The teacher attempts to use assessment results to make data-driven decisions targeted toward improving student achievement but is only **partially successful**.	The teacher **does not** consistently and effectively use assessment results to make data-driven decisions targeted toward improving student achievement.

DEADLINES FOR TASK COMPLETION

Book Study Group Meeting #1: Date: _____ Time: _____
Location: _____
Book Study Group Meeting #2: Date: _____ Time: _____
Location: _____
Book Study Group Meeting #3: Date: _____ Time: _____
Location: _____
Video Analysis #1: Date: _____ Video Analysis #2: Date: _____
Student Survey #1: Date: _____ Student Survey #2: Date: _____
Portfolio Due Date: _____

STUDENT SURVEY—ELEMENTARY VERSION
CLASSROOM INSTRUCTION

Date: _____ Class Period: _____

Directions: Please read the statements below. For each statement place an X in the box that identifies how much you agree with that statement. **Do not write your name on this survey**. When everyone has completed this survey, the forms will be collected and reviewed by your teacher. Your teacher will not know who completed each individual survey.

Table 4.2. K-5 Assessment Survey

Statement	Strongly Agree	Agree	Disagree	Strongly Disagree
My teacher tells me what I do right and what I do wrong on assignments that are graded.				
My teacher's comments help me know what I can do better next time.				
Tests and quizzes are fair.				
I try to do my best on graded assignments.				
After receiving a grade on an assignment, we get additional work to help us learn what we did not know.				
My teacher knows what I don't understand about what he or she is teaching.				

STUDENT SURVEY—SECONDARY VERSION
CLASSROOM INSTRUCTION

Date: _____ Class Period: _____

Directions: Please read the statements below. For each statement place an X in the box that identifies your level of agreement with that statement. **Do not write your name on this survey.** When everyone has completed this survey, the forms will be collected and reviewed by your teacher. Your teacher will not know who completed each individual survey.

Table 4.3. 6-12 Assessment Survey

Statement	Strongly Agree	Agree	Disagree	Strongly Disagree
My teacher provides with me feedback on graded assignments that helps me understand what I did well and what I can do better.				
My teacher's comments on graded assignments help me to improve on future assignments.				
The content of tests and quizzes represents what we have spent the most time learning.				
I am motivated to do my best on graded assignments.				
After receiving a grade on an assignment, we get additional instruction or activities designed to improve what we did not do well.				
After receiving a grade on an assignment, we get additional instruction or activities designed to extend what we have already learned.				
My teacher has an accurate understanding of the content I understand and do not understand.				

STUDENT SURVEY SUMMARY (FORM 1)

Teacher's Name: _____ School Year: _____

Grade: _____ Subject: _____

Survey Version Given: _____ Elementary _____ Secondary

Student Response Analysis

1. Describe the grade level, subject area, and number of students:

2. List any factors that might have influenced the responses:

3. What did students perceive as your strengths?

4. What did students perceive as your weaknesses?

5. What, if anything, do you need to do differently as a result of these responses?

STUDENT SURVEY SUMMARY (FORM 2)

Teacher's Name: _____ School Year: _____

Grade: _____ Subject: _____

Survey Version Given: _____ Elementary _____ Secondary

Student Response Analysis

1. List any factors that might have influenced the responses:

2. What did students perceive as your strengths?

3. What did students perceive as your weaknesses?

4. What, if anything, changed significantly since the first time you administered the student survey?

PORTFOLIO—YEAR THREE CLASSROOM ASSESSMENT

This portfolio is a collection of your work. It represents you and the work that you have done during this school year. Some of the work will need to be selected, while other work will need to be created for this portfolio. For work which you select, staple on top a cover sheet that explains to the reader **what the selection is**, **what you thought of it**, **what you learned from it**, and anything else you would like to include. Each cover sheet must be between one and three paragraphs.

1. **COVER LETTER**: Give the reader an introduction to you and your portfolio. Include **one separate paragraph** for each of the following:
   a. Describe how you regularly communicate to students the level of progress they are making in your class.
   b. Describe the process you use to assemble a formative assessment.
   c. Describe how you use data from assessments to make instructional decisions.
   d. Describe how you make and communicate summative judgments regarding student progress.
2. **REQUIRED ELEMENTS:**
   a. Student Survey Summary Forms 1 and 2
3. **CHOICES** (Be sure to include a cover sheet for each choice.)
   a. Choose an assessment table for a summative assessment.
   b. Choose a performance-based task with the corresponding rubric.
   c. Choose a summative assessment that represents multiple question types.
4. **PRESENTATION**:
   a. Include a table of contents and make sure your work is submitted in order.

(Staple to inside front cover of manila folder.)

Table 4.4. Portfolio Assessment Rubric

	PORTFOLIO ASSESSMENT FORM			
	SCORE 3.0	SCORE 2.0	SCORE 1.0	SCORE 0
COVER LETTER	Five separate paragraphs each of which meets **all** of the specified requirements.	Five separate paragraphs, each of which meets **most** of the specified requirements.	Five separate paragraphs, each of which meets **some** of the specified requirements.	No cover letter included or missing entire required sections.
REQUIRED ELEMENTS	All of the elements required are submitted. The reflection for each item is thoughtful and comprehensive.	All of the elements required are submitted, however at least some aspects of the reflections are superficial.	Some of the required elements are submitted.	None of the required elements are submitted.
CHOICES	Three items selected, each of which has a cover sheet that meets **all** of the specified requirements.	Three items selected, each of which has a cover sheet that meets **most** of the specified requirements.	Three items selected, each of which has a cover sheet that meets **some** of the specified requirements.	Missing one or more of the required choices.

TOTAL SCORE: _____/9

(Staple to inside rear cover of manila folder.)

TEACHER SUMMATIVE EVALUATION REPORT

Teacher: _____ Academic Year: _____

Table 4.5. Assessment Performance Rubric Ratings

SUBDOMAIN	PROFICIENT	DEVELOPING	BEGINNING
Feedback	The teacher **consistently and effectively** provides students with high-quality feedback on performance.	The teacher attempts to provide students with high-quality feedback but is only **partially successful**.	The teacher **does not** consistently and effectively provide students with high-quality feedback.
Assessment Strategies	The teacher **consistently and effectively** uses research-based strategies to gather accurate information about student achievement.	The teacher attempts to use research-based strategies to gather accurate information about student achievement but is only **partially successful**.	The teacher **does not** consistently and effectively use research-based strategies to gather accurate information about student achievement.
Data Use	The teacher **consistently and effectively** uses assessment results to make data-driven decisions targeted toward improving student achievement.	The teacher attempts to use assessment results to make data-driven decisions targeted toward improving student achievement but is only **partially successful**.	The teacher **does not** consistently and effectively use assessment results to make data-driven decisions targeted toward improving student achievement.
PREVIOUS DOMAINS	PERFORMANCE RATING		
DOMAIN 1—Classroom Management	Continues to meet expectations	Does not continue to meet expectations	
DOMAIN 2—Classroom Instruction	Continues to meet expectations	Does not continue to meet expectations	
DOMAIN 4—Professionalism	Continues to meet expectations	Does not continue to meet expectations	

Comments:

Teacher's Signature: _____ Date: _____
Evaluator's Signature: _____ Date: _____

5

Year Four: Teacher Action Research

Teachers demonstrating proficiency with the knowledge and skills of this systematic induction program will have established a solid foundation for future success. They will know how to manage a classroom, deliver direct instruction, assess student learning, and demonstrate professionalism. Yet due to the complexity of the craft, learning to teach is a life-long endeavor. The most experienced teachers acknowledge, frequently with pride, that they are still perfecting their craft long after their initial years in the classroom.

Professionals' capacity to make professional judgments takes between four and eight years to develop (Schon, 1987). Thus, teachers entering their fourth year are entering a critical phase in their development. They are learning to make judgments at a more expert level.

In other words, teachers at this phase of their career development will be solidifying their instructional approaches, assessment strategies, and classroom management practices. Yet, this is also a phase in which teacher motivation can become an issue.

As teachers progress in their career development, they can become less motivated (West, 2012). Achievement of technical competence frequently begins to give way to focus on the value and purpose of teaching. Without purposeful professional engagement, teachers can become disillusioned and feel isolated. In short, at this stage in their careers teachers need to share their struggles with student behavior and instructional approaches, as well as keep their focus on the future in a positive way.

How does a school or district facilitate this teacher transition? One strategy with great promise is teacher action research. Teacher action research is the planned methodical study of one's own teaching. The overarching goal of teacher action research is the collection of valid information that can be used to make informed, rather than intuitive, decisions. There are many models of implementation of teacher action research, but most include the following steps.

First, the teacher identifies an area of concern or interest. After doing a review of existing literature, the teacher develops a problem statement and at least one research question. To answer the research question, the teacher identifies an action plan and methods for data collection. After implementing the appropriate strategies and collecting the data, the teacher conducts an analysis and draws conclusions. These conclusions and their corresponding implications for practice are then shared with colleagues.

Even though the steps have been listed sequentially, the process is frequently recursive. Often there is repetition or alteration of steps based on how the study is progressing. In addition, the lengths of studies vary based on the nature of the problem identified. It is not a one-size-fits-all approach.

Teacher action research has been proven to increase teacher knowledge directly related to classroom practice (Sagor, 1992). In this case, teachers will build upon and extend their knowledge of the content introduced throughout the novice phase of the induction program. Teachers will continue interacting with previously introduced content, but in different ways. Thus, teachers transitioning from the novice to professional level will continue expanding and consolidating their pedagogical repertoire.

Furthermore, teacher action research promotes and expands upon the type of reflective thinking that was required during the novice phase of the induction program. Throughout the novice phase, teachers were required to analyze student survey data as well as videotaped segments of classroom practice. In addition, they compiled portfolios requiring metacognitive thought. Done effectively, teacher action research results in the understanding that good teachers are good students. They are lifelong learners seeking to improve their knowledge and practice throughout their careers.

Teacher action research addresses motivational concerns. It is a professional growth activity that fosters ownership of effective practice as well as an openness to new ideas. Additionally, by its nature, teacher action research promotes collegiality focused on substantive issues. Lastly, teacher action research promotes professionalism through the expectation that teachers will interact with and contribute to the development of the professional knowledge base. They are no longer expected to simply serve as consumers of other people's research.

Of course, as with virtually all professional growth activities, administrative leadership and support is vital to the success of teacher action research. Time for problem-solving and collaboration is essential. If teachers at a grade level or within a department are conducting a collaborative action research project, they will require more meeting time than is needed for a project being completed individually. Yet even an individually conducted project benefits from time for a teacher to brainstorm and dialogue with colleagues. Part of the power of the action research process is the reflective dialogue it requires.

Administrators must provide a forum for sharing the results from these studies. Sharing results of locally conducted studies is highly relevant to other staff members. The fact that these studies are done in the context of the local school or district increases the chances that other faculty members are experiencing similar issues. Therefore, findings in one teacher's classroom may have a positive impact on results in other teachers' classrooms. Furthermore, as a result of learning about a colleague's research, faculty members may acquire new ideas for further research of their own.

Sharing results can take many forms. The school or district could publish and distribute their own academic journal comprised of completed studies. On professional development days, projects could be shared through poster sessions. At faculty meetings, staff can share their research and findings via PowerPoint presentations. Providing forums for sharing signifies the value of both the research and the researcher.

Those leading teachers in the implementation of action research projects must provide the basic knowledge and skills required to successfully complete the process. In addition, they must provide clear expectations regarding project parameters, deadlines, and final products. In the next section of this chapter, the basic competencies required to implement a project will be detailed. Also provided will be a sample completed proposal and project report. Timelines and templates must be adjusted to meet local requirements and resources. All of this information can be copied, distributed, and then reviewed with the appropriate faculty members near the start of implementing teacher action research.

Chapter 5

OVERVIEW OF YEAR FOUR

Welcome to year four of our district's teacher induction program. The goal for this year will be for you to continue demonstrating proficiency in the areas of classroom management, instruction, assessment, and professionalism. Instead of consuming and applying knowledge, you will be provided an opportunity to produce knowledge through the systematic study of your own classroom practices. In addition, you will be sharing the results of your study with your colleagues. The content of the following handbook is intended to serve as your guide for this process. Your project will be evaluated through the use of the following rubric.

TEACHER ACTION RESEARCH PROJECT RUBRIC

Your **research proposal** is due to your immediate supervisor on:

_____

Your **research report** is due to your immediate supervisor on:

_____

Table 5.1. Teacher Action Research Project Rating Rubrics

Project Components	Proficient	Developing	Beginning
Literature Review	The literature review includes a wide variety of appropriate sources related to the area of interest.	The literature review is limited in scope.	No literature review has been conducted or the literature review is unrelated to the areas of interest.
Problem Statement	The problem statement includes who is impacted, what is suspected of causing the problem, the kind of problem it is, the goal for improvement, and what the researcher proposes to do about it.	The problem statement is missing one or two of the required elements.	The problem statement is missing three or more of the required elements.
Research Question	The research question is appropriately narrow, requires higher-level thinking, is precise, avoids ambiguous terms, and can be answered by the researcher within any time constraints established.	The research question is overly broad and/or contains ambiguous terms.	The research question can be answered with a yes or no answer and/or is not answerable by the researcher.
Data Collection	At least three sources of appropriate data are identified for answering the research question.	The scope of data sources identified for answering the research question is inadequate.	There are no data sources identified for answering the research question or the data sources are completely unrelated to the research question.

(continued)

Table 5.1. (*continued*)

Project Components	Proficient	Developing	Beginning
Implementation Plan	A logical sequence of steps for the intervention is articulated and a sensible timeline is identified.	The steps for the intervention plan are illogical and/or the timeline provided does not make sense.	The implementation plan is either not presented or is incomprehensible.
Data Analysis	The narrative summary of the data analysis is comprehensive and logical.	The narrative summary of the data analysis is limited and/or does not make sense.	The narrative summary of the data analysis is either not presented or is incomprehensible.
Conclusions	The tentative conclusions make sense based on the data analysis.	It is difficult to determine how the data supports the conclusions presented.	The tentative conclusions are not presented.
Reporting Results	The implications for classroom practice are clearly articulated and logical future research questions have been identified.	Implications for practice are unclear and/or future research questions do not make sense.	Implications for practice and/or future research questions are not presented.

TEACHER ACTION RESEARCH HANDBOOK

1. What is teacher action research?
   a. Teacher action research is **planned, methodical** observation related to **one's own teaching**.
2. What are the benefits of conducting teacher action research?
   a. Assists teachers in developing new knowledge directly related to their own classrooms.
   b. Encourages informed rather than intuitive decision-making about classroom practices.
   c. Empowers teachers to make decisions regarding areas of interest and need.
   d. Encourages collegial dialogue focused on substantive issues of teaching and learning.
3. What are the steps in conducting teacher action research?
   a. Step One—Identify an Area of Interest or Concern
      i. Teacher action research begins with asking: What elements of practice or what aspects of student learning do I wish to examine in depth?
      ii. Regardless of the area of interest selected, it must concern the teaching/learning process and be within the teacher's scope of influence.
   b. Step Two—Review Relevant Literature
      i Explore a range of books, articles, and reports related to your topic. Doing so will increase your knowledge of what is already known about the topic. In addition, reading relevant literature on your chosen topic may also give you ideas for instructional strategies.
      ii. Appropriate resources from the list provided in the appendix of this document can be examined related to various aspects of the content presented in the first phase of the teacher induction program.
   c. Step Three—Develop a Problem Statement
      i. Having conducted a thorough review of the literature in your area of interest, the next step is the development of a problem statement. Establishing a clear idea of what you are studying and why you are studying it is a critical step toward successful completion of any action research proj-

ect. Composing a problem statement of approximately 100 words that is clear and concise focuses the remainder of the work. Your problem statement contains answers to the following questions:
1. Who is impacted?
2. Who or what is suspected of causing the problem?
3. What kind of problem is it? (resources, skills, time, materials, etc.)
4. What is the goal for improvement?
5. What do you propose to do about it?

Example problem statement—My students are not correctly editing the final drafts of their written work (*answers questions 1 and 3*). I believe this is due to the fact that they are not using effective editing strategies (*answers question 2*). I want all students to provide final drafts that are free of grade-level grammar and spelling errors (*answers question 4*). Therefore, I will train my students and then require them to use an editing checklist (*answers question 5*).

d. **Step Four—Develop a Research Question**
   i. Even though no perfect formula exists for framing an action research question, many teachers find it helpful to use the following framework. "What is the impact of _____ on _____?" In the first blank the practice is described. The second blank names the desired impact. A research question that could be used for the above problem statement is "What is the impact of using editing checklists on the quantity of grammar and spelling errors in final drafts?"
   ii. Regardless of the format used, quality teacher action research questions are appropriately narrow, require higher level thinking (not yes or no answers), are precise, avoid ambiguous terms, and can be answered by the researcher within any time constraints established. A question should be revised until it meets these criteria.

e. **Step Five—Data Collection**
   i. Before implementing any instructional interventions, the action researcher must decide the type of data required to answer their research question. They must also determine

how they will systematically collect that data as well as the time frame they will follow for data collection. There are many types of data that an action researcher can collect. Types of data can be categorized as either:
1. Quantitative—data that can be measured by numbers.
2. Qualitative—data that can be measured by descriptions. The choice of the type of data collected will depend upon the research question. A list of data collection instruments can be found in the appendix to this document.

   ii. To increase the validity and reliability of findings, action researchers strive to triangulate their data. Triangulation involves collecting multiple sources of data for every phenomenon or issue being studied. Triangulation of data compensates for the imperfections of single data-gathering instruments, thus increasing confidence in results. Triangulation can be achieved by collecting the same type of data over time or by collecting different types of data on the same phenomenon of interest.

f. Step Six—Implementation Plan
   i. Reviewing the literature will likely have provided you with ideas for new techniques and strategies that you think will produce better results. At this stage in the process, it is important to list both the steps and timeline for implementing the identified intervention(s). Taking this action will make your intervention capable of being repeated by others and will keep you focused on the appropriate implementation procedures.

g. Step Seven—Data Analysis
   i. Once the data has been collected it must be organized. If the data is quantitative, then tables and graphs can be used to create a visual display. If the data is qualitative, a matrix can be created to organize the data by categories.

   ii. As you "interrogate" the data, you are looking for the patterns or themes that emerge. Once you identify these patterns or themes, the next step is to categorize the data from your study that supports each one. You are now ready to draw tentative conclusions.

h. **Step Eight—Reporting Results**
   i When reporting results, your audience is your fellow educators. The goals of sharing what you have learned are to share your tentative conclusions and the implications those conclusions have for classroom practice. It is absolutely acceptable for your conclusions to be different than what you had expected. Sometimes we learn just as much from what did not work as what did. In fact, this often leads to additional questions for further research. Articulating potential questions for future research is the final step in reporting the results of a teacher action research project.
   ii. As described up to this point, teacher action research appears to be a linear process. Often it is not sequential. Instead, it is often recursive with revisions, adjustments, and revisiting previous steps throughout the study. This fluidity is the nature of the action research process.
4. Implementation Process
   a. Staff will complete and submit the template "Teacher Action Research Proposal" by the deadline provided. This template serves as an organizer for the planning phase of your teacher action research project. The content of this template will be reviewed and either approved or sent back for revisions. Minor changes to plans after approval, such as tweaking the language of the research question or reordering the steps of the implementation plan, do not need to be resubmitted. Major changes like a change in the interest area or a complete revision of the problem statement must be resubmitted for approval.
   b. Staff will collect data, implement their plan, analyze their data, and draw their tentative conclusions, including implications and potential future research questions. Opportunities for assistance and consultation will be provided at various times throughout the implementation of the projects.
   c. The "Teacher Action Research Report" template will serve as the organizing framework for reporting the results. Submission of research report results must occur by the deadline provided. Submitted work will be reviewed for completion.
   d. A description of how results will be shared with colleagues will be provided. It is expected that every teacher researcher will share their results with the rest of the faculty.

SAMPLE TEACHER ACTION RESEARCH PROPOSAL

Table 5.2. Sample Teacher Action Research Proposal

Staff Member's Name: Jane Doe **School Year:** 2020–2021

I will be working to implement this plan: ___X___ Individually _____ In a Group.
If in a group, please list group members:

PROBLEM IDENTIFICATION

INTEREST AREA: Fluency with single-digit multiplication facts.

LITERATURE REVIEWED:
Lang-Raad, N. D., & Marzano, R. J. (2019). *The new art and science of teaching mathematics*. Bloomington, IN: Solution Tree.
Sousa, D. A. (2014). *How the brain learns mathematics*. Thousand Oaks, CA: Corwin.

PROBLEM STATEMENT:
My students are not demonstrating fluency with single-digit multiplication. I believe this is due to the fact that they are not participating in short, focused, and regular distributed practice sessions. I want all students to develop automaticity with multiplication facts. Therefore, I will implement a "Mad Minute" for multiplication as a daily warm-up for math class.

RESEARCH QUESTION:
What is the impact of daily, one-minute multiplication practice on automaticity with single-digit multiplication facts?

DATA COLLECTION METHODS

DATA SOURCE #1 (What & How) Pre-assessment of single-digit multiplication administered prior to implementation of one-minute multiplication practice sessions.

DATA SOURCE #2 (What & How) Students will graph daily how many facts they got correct.

DATA SOURCE #3 (What & How) Post-assessment of single-digit multiplication administered upon conclusion of implementation of one-minute multiplication practice sessions.

(continued)

Table 5.2. *(continued)*

IMPLEMENTATION SCHEDULE	
TASKS	**TIMELINE**
Administer pre-assessment.	November 1, 2020
Implement daily one-minute multiplication practice sessions at the beginning of each math class. Teach students to record results.	November 2, 2020
Administer post-assessment.	December 23, 2020

Initial Approval: _____ **(Supervisor's Signature)** _____
(Date)

TEACHER ACTION RESEARCH REPORT

Teacher Name: Jane Doe

School Year: 2020–2021

Teacher's Signature: _____ Date: _____

Supervisor's Signature: _____ Date: _____

Table 5.3. Sample Teacher Action Research Report

DATA ANALYSIS
Provide a narrative summary of your collected and analyzed data. If appropriate, please attach graphs and tables to this summary.
After administering the pre-test, I compiled the range, mean, and median for the class. The class average for the number of correct facts completed in 60 seconds was 23. However, the range was from 3 to 46. Thus, the median of 31 correct facts was a more accurate reflection of class performance. During the intervention, students recorded and graphed daily results. These results were reviewed weekly. Analysis of these weekly graphs revealed that 78% of the students demonstrated an increased number of facts correct every week. Of this 78%, the majority (61%) demonstrated an increase of 3 or more correct facts weekly. Of the 22% of the students that did not demonstrate a weekly increase of facts correct, all but two of them demonstrated an increase in at least half of the weeks. Two of the students did not demonstrate consistent growth in any of the weeks. The administered post-test was again analyzed for the range, mean, and median. The range of this data set went from 5 to 67. The average number of correct facts was 39. The median for this data set was 46, which is much closer to the mean than the pre-test data set.

CONCLUSIONS
Describe your tentative conclusions from your data analysis.
Daily single-digit multiplication fluency drills improve automaticity with math facts for the majority of students.
Some students do not achieve increased automaticity of single-digit multiplication facts with daily fluency drills.

(continued)

Table 5.3. *(continued)*

IMPLICATIONS

Describe the importance of your findings for teaching and learning in our school.

If incorporated into our mathematics program, daily fluency drills have the potential to increase automaticity with single-digit multiplication facts. This was achieved with minimal expenditure of class time and no new resources purchased.

Describe future research you or others could do as a follow up to this study.

Why did a small number of students not achieve increased automaticity as a result of this practice?

Will the increased automaticity with single-digit multiplication continue without this intervention?

Results

_____ **Project Requirements met.**

_____ **Project Requirements not met.**

Comments:

6

The Role of Mentoring in the Induction Program

For mentoring to be successful it must be one part of a larger structured induction process. According to Smith and Ingersoll (2004), the support of a mentor alone is a practice that only reduces five-year teacher attrition rates by one percentage point. Yet, as one part of an overall induction program, mentoring can help novice teachers face the challenges of teaching. Mentors can engage mentees through reflective activities and professional conversations as well as providing social-emotional support.

Additionally, mentoring can foster the professional development of mentors. Mentoring encourages veteran teachers to improve themselves, receive respect, develop collegiality, and profit from novice teachers' fresh ideas and energy. Done properly, mentoring has benefits for both the mentor and the mentee (Breaux, 2016).

To be clear, there is nothing beneficial about a haphazard mentoring process. If it is to be effective, a mentoring program must be focused and structured. More specifically there must be a systematic selection process, clarity regarding roles and responsibilities, adequate training to meet those responsibilities, and time for collaboration.

Unfortunately, mentors are often chosen for the wrong reasons. It may be that they are the willing volunteers or those who seek financial compensation for performing the role. Perhaps little thought is given to the selection of the mentor. Yet having no mentor is better than having an ineffective one. If we want new teachers to be effective and to stay in teaching, then only our most effective teachers should be selected for the mentoring role.

In addition, a person with an attitude that falls short of true professionalism should never serve as a mentor for a new teacher. Even if they are a good teacher within the walls of their own classroom, the damage they do to a new teacher's attitude toward teaching can be long lasting and pervasive. Regardless of the process used to select mentors, the goal should be to select the best and only the best for this role.

Mentors must have a clear understanding of their roles and responsibilities. A mentor teacher is one who serves as a role model. Through their example, they demonstrate how to handle difficult conversations and sensitive situations.

Mentors serve as informal guides as to how things work within a school and a district. They guide novice teachers in completing the multitude of procedures required in the regular operation of schools. They also help novice teachers understand the unwritten norms for behavior that exist within a school.

Novice teachers require emotional support. The first years of teaching are stressful and can be overwhelming. Through a trusting relationship characterized by active listening and encouragement, mentor teachers can provide this support. The relationship between a mentor and a mentee cannot be stressed enough. A new teacher has to trust a mentor enough to share both successes and mistakes.

One of the more overwhelming aspects of being a novice teacher is the lack of guidance and resources they receive for instructional planning. Forty-one percent of first-year teachers surveyed nationwide stated that their schools or districts provide them with few or no instructional resources (Mathews, 2011).

Although such curricular freedom may be cherished by veteran teachers, it is a burden for new teachers. Novice teachers have yet to develop a robust repertoire of lesson ideas and instructional materials. A mentor can provide these resources through sharing instructional plans and proven classroom materials. Of course, this is much easier to do if the mentor and mentee share the same content area and/or grade level for instruction.

Lastly, novice teachers yearn for, but seldom receive, meaningful feedback on their instructional practices from veteran colleagues (McCormack, Gore, & Thomas, 2006). Regrettably Fry (2007) found that mentor teachers assigned to provide this support were sometimes part of the problem. He concluded that mentors dispensed little guidance, if not bad advice. Properly trained mentors can provide coaching through the modeling of effective strategies and objective observations of mentee's instruction.

Knowing how to teach and knowing how to teach someone else to teach are two very different skill sets. To be effective, mentors need knowledge of how to support new teachers and skill at providing guidance. In addition, mentor teachers need support and the opportunity to discuss other ideas, problems, and solutions with other mentor teachers.

Finally, mentor teachers need time to both observe and reflect upon instruction with their mentees. Perhaps they have reduced teaching loads or substitute coverage is provided in order to complete their mentoring responsibilities. It is counterproductive to make serving as a mentor an overwhelming task. Without time, mentors and mentees will become frustrated, making it very difficult to build the types of supportive relationships that benefit both the mentor and the new teacher.

The section that follows is a handbook that can be provided to mentor teachers. This handbook can serve as the basis for a training program or a supplement to an already existing one. It is intended to be a guide for how mentor teachers can serve as supports for new teachers throughout the previously described induction process.

MENTOR HANDBOOK

Congratulations on being chosen to mentor a novice teacher. This selection is a testament to your high level of professionalism and your instructional expertise. Mentoring a novice teacher is both an awesome opportunity and a major responsibility. As a mentor you will be expected to fill the following roles:

- Role Model
- Guide
- Caring Colleague
- Resource
- Coach

Your words and actions will make a significant impression on the novice teacher you are mentoring. What you say and how you act will serve as the model that shapes their professional behavior. This will be especially true when you are handling difficult or sensitive situations. You were chosen for this role because the district believes you set the example that we seek for our staff members.

As their guide you will be helping the novice teacher understand the multitude of procedures required for the operation of our school and district. Things that veteran teachers may take for granted are brand new to the novice teacher. Everything from making photocopies to scheduling parent-teacher conferences will need some degree of explanation. Furthermore, you will be essential for helping the novice teacher navigate the social relationships that exist within your building.

At the core of mentoring is the relationship between the mentor and the new teacher. Trust is the determining factor that will make this relationship either flourish or perish. A new teacher needs to trust a mentor enough to share both their successes and their mistakes without judgment. Your mentee needs to be assured that you will keep all of the communications between the two of you private. Even speaking of the mentee in a complimentary way shouldn't be done without first asking their permission. Trust can be difficult to establish, but it can be easily destroyed.

Furthermore, the novice must understand that you are not there to evaluate or judge them. Instead, they must believe that you are there to help them—and only help them. Additionally, they need to understand that you will do everything within reason to help them succeed.

As a mentor you will serve as an invaluable instructional resource. Novice teachers do not have years of instructional plans, materials, and resources to draw from. In fact, they often do not yet know what will and will not work in their classroom. You can provide them with model plans to follow and share your classroom materials and resources. Furthermore, you can direct them to where they can find additional resources both within and outside the school. Even better, if possible, you can collaborate with the novice teacher to develop plans. They will benefit greatly from learning how a professional teacher prepares for instruction.

The final role you will assume is that of an instructional coach. Reviewing the content of the book *From First Year to First Rate* (Jennings, 2021) with them will help the novice teacher deepen their understanding of the critical components of effective teaching. In addition, inviting them to observe your use of any of these strategies will provide the novice teacher with a real-life example of effective implementation. Lastly, observing their use of these strategies will provide you with the opportunity to provide feedback the novice teacher can use for growth.

Mentoring Skills

Knowing how to teach and teaching someone else to teach are two very different skills. This section is intended to provide you with the basic skills you require to mentor effectively. The first and perhaps most important skills required are interpersonal. An interpersonal skill that will build trust and encourage the mentee to express him or herself freely is active listening.

Active listening is hard work, because we usually only listen long enough to hear what we need to make our next point of agreement or disagreement. Follow these recommendations to improve your active listening skills:

- Refrain from interrupting the person speaking; don't be afraid of silence.
- If there is not enough time to listen actively, say so.
- Paraphrase: listen to what is being said without distraction, then summarize what you have heard and understood (example: "I think I hear you saying that you are frustrated by the amount of time it takes students to line up for recess.").
- Check with the speaker to make sure that your interpretation of what you have heard is correct (example: "It sounds like you don't think your students are motivated to complete their homework. Is that correct?").
- Probe to expand on ideas, unearth assumptions, and explore applications (example: "Help me understand what led you to that conclusion?").
- Be aware of your nonverbal behaviors. Making eye contact communicates interest and helps you establish rapport. Smiling indicates warmth and openness in communication. Good posture conveys poise and confidence.

Another skill that is required to be an effective mentor is providing quality feedback. It stands to reason that if a teacher does not know what he or she is doing right or wrong, it will be difficult for them to improve their knowledge or skill. To improve the quality of feedback you provide, practice the following behaviors:

- Be honest and genuine, but say what you mean without being mean. Tact is important.
- Avoid overwhelming the mentee. It is better to offer advice in small doses and work on one area for improvement at a time. One small success at a time will lead to bigger victories as the teacher's skill level and knowledge increases.
- Be descriptive (example: "When you were presenting instruction, three of the students were viewing their phones.") instead of evaluative (example: "Your instructional presentation skills were boring.").
- Be future oriented. Specify the strategies a teacher is performing correctly and effectively as well as which strategies require changes moving forward because they were demonstrated with errors or omissions. You can also provide feedback on strategies a teacher could have used in the lesson but didn't. This will give them ideas for future lessons.

Conducting Classroom Visitations with Your Mentee

One situation in which you will have to provide feedback is the observation of your mentee's teaching. The process for observation will be guided by the protocols provided below. The mentee will complete the pre-observation conference protocol form. You will then meet to discuss the contents of this form and establish how data will be collected. During your observation you will collect student and teacher evidence related to the focus of the observation. Shortly after the observation you will make notes and list ideas or questions for discussion. Lastly, you will meet and discuss the observation using the post-conference protocol procedure.

COACHING FORMS
PRE-OBSERVATION CONFERENCE PROTOCOL

This section is to be completed by the mentee in advance of the pre-observation meeting:

- What is the objective for this lesson?

- What specifically do you want me to look for?

- Is there anything specific you want me to know about this class or lesson prior to the observation?

- When will the observation be and for how long will it take place?

- When and where will we meet after the observation to reflect upon the lesson?

COACHING OBSERVATION FORM

Date: _____ Time: _____

Teacher's Name: _____ Observer: _____

Instructional Focus:

Table 6.1. Teacher and Student Evidence

TEACHER EVIDENCE	STUDENT EVIDENCE
OBSERVATION NOTES	**IDEAS AND QUESTIONS**

POST-OBSERVATION CONFERENCE PROTOCOL

- Mentee describes how he or she thinks the lesson went.
- Based upon the focus area for the observation, discuss what the mentor observed.
- Collaborative reflection on the observations—what does the gathered data mean?
- Collaborative discussion of observation results for future practice. What can the mentee do differently to improve and how can he or she do it?

In addition to observing your mentee's instruction, there are several other activities you can complete to coach them. These activities relate directly to the induction program requirements. They include:

- Your mentee is required to create and submit a portfolio. You can assist them with selecting and reflecting upon their documents and then review the portfolio with them prior to submission.
- Your mentee is required to record and reflect upon video of their teaching. With their permission, you can watch the recording with them and assist them with the required reflection.
- Your mentee is required to collect and analyze student survey data. You can review and discuss this data with them.

Thank you for agreeing to serve as a mentor. Your work will have a tremendous impact on your mentee and on our school district. We encourage your suggestions and feedback to assist us with continually improving the structure necessary to help our novice teachers succeed.

Teachers demonstrating proficiency with the content of this induction program will have established a solid foundation for long-term career success. They will have engaged in a multitude of reflective activities designed to lead to mastery of the basic components of teaching. In short, they will have reached the professional stage of their teaching careers.

Of course, professional growth should not end here. Instead, teachers should be encouraged to continue their teacher action research and learn about more advanced instructional techniques. Professional teachers have the mastery of basic classroom management, instruction, and assessment required to become effective with more advanced teaching strategies like problem-based learning and high-quality group work.

After serving in the capacity of a professional teacher for several years, these teachers may be prepared and inclined to take on roles of teacher leadership. In those roles they will be able to facilitate the growth of their peers through such activities as data coaching, providing professional development activities, and leading teams. Teaching is a never-ending quest for continuous growth and improvement. It is our responsibility as school and district leaders to provide teachers with differentiated opportunities that match their needs and abilities.

Appendix

ACTION RESEARCH LITERATURE REVIEW SUGGESTIONS

Glass, K. T., & Marzano, R. J. (2018). *The new art and science of teaching writing*. Bloomington, IN: Solution Tree.

Hattie, J. (2012). *Visible learning for teachers: Maximizing impact on learning*. London and New York: Routledge.

Hunter, R. (2004). *Mastery teaching: Increasing instructional effectiveness in elementary and secondary schools*. Thousand Oaks, CA: Corwin.

Lang-Raad, N. D., & Marzano, R. J. (2019). *The new art and science of teaching mathematics*. Bloomington, IN: Solution Tree.

Marzano, R. J. (2004). *Building background knowledge for academic achievement: Research on what works in schools*. Alexandria, VA: Association for Supervision and Curriculum Development.

———. (2006). *Classroom assessment and grading that work*. Alexandria, VA: Association for Supervision and Curriculum Development.

———. (2009). *Designing and teaching learning goals and objectives*. Bloomington, IN: Marzano Research Laboratory.

———. (2009). *Formative assessment and standards-based grading*. Bloomington, IN: Marzano Research Laboratory.

———. (2017). *Making classroom assessments reliable and valid*. Bloomington, IN: Solution Tree.

———. (2017). *The new art and science of teaching*. Bloomington, IN: Solution Tree.

Marzano, R. J., Marzano, J. S., & Pickering, D. J. (2003). *Classroom management that works: Research-based strategies for every teacher*. Alexandria, VA: Association for Supervision and Curriculum Development.

Marzano, R. J., & Norford, J. S. (2018). *The new art and science of classroom assessment*. Bloomington, IN: Solution Tree.

Marzano, R. J., & Pickering, D. J. (2010). *The highly engaged classroom.* Bloomington, IN: Marzano Research Laboratory.

Marzano, R. J., & Simms, J. A. (2014). *Questioning sequences in the classroom.* Bloomington, IN: Marzano Research Laboratory.

Onuscheck, M., Marzano, R. J., & Grice, J. (2019). *The new art and science of teaching art and music.* Bloomington, IN: Solution Tree.

Popham, W. J. (2003). *Test better, teach better: The instructional role of assessment.* New York: Houghton Mifflin Harcourt.

———. (2008). *Transformative assessment.* Alexandria, VA: Association for Supervision and Curriculum Development.

Simms, J. A., & Marzano, R. J. (2018). *The new art and science of teaching reading.* Bloomington, IN: Solution Tree.

Sousa, D. A. (2015). *Brain-friendly assessments: What they are and how to use them.* West Palm Beach, FL: Learning Sciences International.

———. (2015). *How the brain influences behavior.* New York: Corwin/Skyhorse.

———. (2016). *How the brain learns.* 5th edition. Thousand Oaks, CA: Corwin.

———. (2014). *How the brain learns mathematics.* Thousand Oaks, CA: Corwin.

———. (2014). *How the brain learns to read.* Thousand Oaks, CA: Corwin.

———. (2010). *How the ELL brain learns.* Thousand Oaks, CA: Corwin.

———. (2009). *How the gifted brain learns.* Thousand Oaks, CA: Corwin.

———. (2014). *How the special needs brain learns.* Thousand Oaks, CA: Corwin.

Appendix

DATA COLLECTION OPTIONS

Table A.1. Data Collection Options for Teacher Action Research

Existing Sources	Tools for Capturing Daily Classroom Experiences	Tools for Questioning
Student Work	Diaries, Logs, Journals	Interviews
Archival Evidence	Videos	Focus Groups
Curriculum-Based Measurements	Photographs	Written Surveys
Student Portfolios	Student Shadowing	
	Observation Checklists/Rating Scales	

TEACHER ACTION RESEARCH PROPOSAL

Table A.2. Teacher Action Research Proposal

Staff Member's Name: School Year:

I will be working to implement this plan: _____ Individually _____ In a Group.
If in a group, please list group members:

PROBLEM IDENTIFICATION

INTEREST AREA:

LITERATURE REVIEWED:

PROBLEM STATEMENT:

RESEARCH QUESTION:

DATA COLLECTION METHODS

DATA SOURCE #1 (What & How)

DATA SOURCE #2 (What & How)

DATA SOURCE #3 (What & How)

IMPLEMENTATION SCHEDULE

TASKS   TIMELINE

Initial Approval: _____ (Supervisor's Signature) _____
(Date) _____

Appendix

TEACHER ACTION RESEARCH REPORT

Teacher Name:

School Year:

Table A.3. Teacher Action Research Report

DATA ANALYSIS
Provide a narrative summary of your collected and analyzed data. If appropriate, please attach graphs and tables to this summary.

CONCLUSIONS
Describe your tentative conclusions from your data analysis.

IMPLICATIONS

Describe the importance of your findings for teaching and learning in our school.

Describe future research you or others could do as a follow-up to this study.

Results

_____ Project requirements met.

_____ Project requirements not met.

Comments:

Teacher Signature:

Date:

Supervisor's Signature:

Date:

References

Aleamoni, L. M. (1999). Student rating myths versus research facts from 1924 to 1998. *Journal of Personnel Evaluation in Education, 13*(2).

Armstrong, V., & Curran, S. (2006). Developing a collaborative model of research using digital video. *Computers and Education, 46*(3).

Breaux, A. (2016). Ten ways to make mentoring work. *Educational Leadership, 73*(8).

Cunningham, A., & Bendetto, S. (2002). Using digital video tools to promote reflective practice. In C. Crawford et al. (Eds.), *Proceedings of Society for Information Technology and Teacher Education International Conference 2002*. Chesapeake, VA: American Association for Computer Education.

Ericsson, K. A. (1996). *The road to excellence: The acquisition of expert performance in the arts and sciences, sports, and games*. Mahwah, NJ: Erlbaum.

Fry, S. W. (2007). *How it's being done: Urgent lessons from unexpected schools*. Cambridge, MA: Harvard Education Press.

Gonzales, F., & Sosa, A. S. (1993, March). How do we keep teachers in our classrooms? The TNT response. *IDRA Newsletter*, 1.

Guin, K. (2004). Chronic teacher turnover in urban elementary schools. *Education Policy Analysis Archives, 12*(42).

Hennessy, S., & Deaney, R. (2009). The impact of collaborative video analysis by practitioners and researchers upon pedagogical thinking and practice: A follow-up study. *Teachers and Teaching: Theory and Practice 15*(5).

Jennings, M. (2021). *From first year to first rate: Thriving during the initial years of your teaching career*. New York: Rowman & Littlefield.

Joyce, B., & Showers, B. (2002). *Student achievement through staff development* (3rd ed.). Alexandria, VA: Association for Supervision and Curriculum Development.

Laitsch, D. (2004) The effects of chronic teacher turnover on school climate and organization. *ACSD ResearchBrief, 2*(19).

Martin, L., Kragler, S., Quatroche, D., & Bauserman, K. (2014). *Handbook of professional development in education*. New York: Guildford.

Marzano, R. J., Boogren, T., Heflebower, T., Kanold-Mcintyre, J., & Pickering, D. (2012). *Becoming a reflective teacher*. Bloomington, IN: Marzano Research Laboratory.

Mathews, J. (2011, December 18). New teacher decries lesson plan gap [blog post]. Retrieved from *Class Struggle* at the *Washington Post*.

McCormack, A., Gore, J., & Thomas, K. (2006). Early career teacher professional learning. *Asia-Pacific Journal of Teacher Education, 34*(1).

Melnick, S. A., & Meister, D. G. (2008). A comparison of beginning and experienced teachers' concerns. *Educational Research Quarterly, 31*(3).

Sagor, R. (1992). *How to conduct collaborative action research*. Alexandria, VA: Association for Supervision and Curriculum Development.

Schon, D. A. (1987). *Educating the reflective practitioner*. San Francisco: Jossey-Bass.

Smith, T. M., & Ingersoll, R. M. (2004). What are the effects of induction and mentoring on beginning teacher turnover? *American Educational Research Journal, 41*(3).

Sorenson, P. D., Newton, L. R., & Harrison, C. (2006). *The professional development of teachers through interaction and digital video*. Paper presented at the British Educational Research Association Annual Conference, Coventry, UK.

West, E. (2012). What are you doing the rest of your life? Strategies for fostering faculty vitality and development mid-career. *Journal of Learning in Higher Education, 8*(1).

About the Author

Matthew Jennings is a twenty-eight-year veteran of education. He has served as a superintendent, assistant superintendent, director of human resources, director of student services, supervisor of curriculum and instruction, and a classroom teacher. He earned his master's degree and doctorate in educational administration from Rutgers University. Dr. Jennings can be reached at mattmarz1994@google.com or through his website https://jennir3.wixsite.com/drjenningsbooks

www.ingramcontent.com/pod-product-compliance
Lightning Source LLC
Chambersburg PA
CBHW020752230426
43665CB00009B/568